YELLOWSTONE SOLITUDE
True Wilderness Encounters

STAN MILLS

Published by Stan Mills
ISBN: 979-8-9947650-0-5

Printed in the United States of America
First Edition

Table of Contents

Prologue

These stories are about my own experiences. They detail my observations and responses during real encounters with grizzly bears. **What follows is not a guide or a set of instructions. It is a record of what I have done and learned, and it should not be taken as advice or as something to be imitated.** I hike alone by choice, and what I share here comes from years of solo travel in wild country. I choose to hike and camp this way because I want to see the wilderness as it truly is, alive with wild creatures going about their lives.

This book follows my solo journey through intact wilderness as it unfolds in real time, capturing what I have observed while moving quietly, attentively, and with calm focus. It portrays grizzly bears not as symbols of danger or chaos, but as aware, responsive animals whose reactions are shaped by human behavior. These accounts reflect knowledge gained through experience, and they also point to a pattern I've noticed: humility, restraint, and awareness often seem to matter more than noise or control.

Choosing to travel alone is central to this journey. Solitude means I cannot rely on the opinions of others; I have to make my own decisions and learn everything through my own experiences. Without distraction, attention sharpens and responsibility feels absolute. Encounters are met as they are, not as the scary stories suggest they should be.

Over time, I have noticed that people tend to approach the wilderness in one of two ways. Some move through it with calm curiosity and respect. Others carry fear with them, even when nothing is happening. Fear can be useful. It keeps us alert and cautious. But when fear dictates every decision, it limits movement, understanding, and life itself.

My own knowledge of grizzly bears did not come quickly. I began cautiously, reading widely and absorbing what others had written. With experience, I learned which ideas held up in the field and which did not. Books provide a starting point, but they cannot replace time spent in the presence of the animals themselves. Understanding grows through repeated encounters, careful observation, and my attempts to keep encounters calm through restraint rather than force.

There are many accounts that emphasize danger and reinforce fear. Far fewer explore what it can look like to move through a bear's world without disturbance. Over time, I have observed that constant noise or defensive behavior has not guaranteed safety for me. What has mattered more has been understanding the animal, recognizing its signs, and maintaining calm during an encounter.

This book is not about bravery, statistics, or proving anything. It is about my experience. It is about observing how animals truly behave, and discovering how our actions shape those encounters. Whether on a remote hillside or a familiar trail, knowledge and attention shape outcomes. The stories that follow reflect that reality.

Hiking Alone in Grizzly Country

I do not hike solo because I dislike people or because I prefer isolation. One reason is that noise changes everything in the backcountry. Avoiding noise from other people is the most obvious part of that, but the effect goes deeper. Noise changes how wildlife behaves, how the landscape feels, and how carefully a person pays attention. Quiet allows me to hear what is happening around me and notice small details that matter.

Bears react to the human voice. That reaction may be a quick retreat, with the bear leaving the area, or it may involve heightened stress that carries greater risk. Either way, the response is rooted in fear. A bear does not hear conversation or laughter as neutral sound, but as an unexpected presence in its home. The situation is similar to a family sitting quietly inside their house when a stranger suddenly crashes through the front door, yelling and creating a commotion. The response in that moment would not be calm or measured. It would be immediate, defensive, and driven by fear. In my view, loud human presence places a grizzly bear in that position, and the risk increases significantly when a mother has cubs and must decide how to protect them while afraid.

When people enter wild places with their attention focused mainly on themselves, it often shows in how they move and behave. Loudness and self-focused movement can feel out of place in an animal's home. For me, the backcountry asks for a different way of being present.

I also choose to hike alone because I do not want the responsibility of being accountable for another person's safety. When another person is present, decisions are no longer based solely on what the land and the animals are communicating. Choices become influenced by another person's pace, expectations, and comfort level. Alone, every decision rests with me. That reality changes how I move and how I think, and it requires focus and humility.

More importantly, my primary concern has always been for the animals and the places they live, not myself alone. I am not interested in imposing myself on the landscape or pushing through it loudly. I want to move in a way that allows animals to continue their routines undisturbed. The goal is to pass through quietly, without forcing movement, flight, or alarm. I do not see myself as the priority.

Solo hiking creates a mindset in which awareness becomes its own form of comfort. Confidence comes from paying attention, not from having someone else nearby. Every sound matters. Every shift in the wind matters. The land holds my full attention, allowing me to move calmly and deliberately, guided by what is actually happening and by years of experience.

Hiking solo in grizzly country is not about bravado or chance for me. It is not learned quickly, and it is not approached casually. In my experience, my sense of safety has depended on three things working together: reading signs, moving with care, and understanding habitat. None of these stands alone. Each depends on the others, and experience with all three is what I rely on to stay safe.

The first piece, for me, has been learning to recognize bear signs. Tracks tell me far more than whether a bear has passed through. They show how recently a bear was there, how many bears may be active in an area, and what kind of bear left the tracks. From tracks, it is often possible to judge what a bear is doing, how fast it is moving, and whether cubs are present which changes the situation completely. Cubs raise concern because of how they may react if they discover me, and because a mother may respond differently while protecting them. Scat adds another layer of information, revealing both how recently bears were present and what food sources they are using.

Scratch marks and rubbing trees matter mainly for their freshness, helping to judge recent activity. Day beds can be difficult to identify and do not always provide clear information. Any single sign can matter, but multiple signs together provide a clearer picture of what is happening in an area.

The second part is movement. Reading signs has little value if movement does not match what the ground is indicating. I stop often. I look. I listen. I pay attention to what can be seen and what cannot be seen. Two things are always at play while moving through the backcountry: the circle of disturbance and the circle of perception.

People moving up a trail yelling "Hey Bear" carries a large circle of disturbance, announcing their presence far beyond what can be seen. By contrast, a deer grazing quietly in a meadow carries a very small circle of disturbance, as does a person who is still, quiet, and deliberate. The circle of perception describes how far away a person can detect or sense what is happening around them. People moving quickly, talking loudly, and focused on each other often have limited awareness of what is around them. A deer that pauses often and regularly lifts its head maintains a wide awareness of what is around it. The same is true for a person who moves slowly, stops often, and remains quiet.

My goal is to move in a way that keeps the circle of disturbance small while allowing the circle of perception to remain large. Wind direction, visibility, vegetation, and terrain all influence that balance. Watching how many people hike in Yellowstone, it is often the opposite. Disturbance is large while awareness is small.

The third part is understanding habitat. Habitat determines whether bears are likely to be present at all. It means knowing how grizzly habitat differs from black bear habitat, and recognizing which areas are likely to hold one or the other. Food is always a primary consideration. When uncertainty arises, the simplest question is often the most useful: What is the food source in this immediate area? The answer can reveal as much as tracks or scat about whether bears are likely to be close. Time of year matters. Daily temperature matters. These factors influence when bears are active and where they are likely to be throughout the day. Taken together, they help me judge the likelihood of bears being in an area, even when there are no visible signs to confirm it.

These three parts cannot be separated. Knowing signs without understanding habitat leaves the picture incomplete. Moving carefully without reading the ground still leaves safety to chance. Understanding habitat without experience in the other two can create a false sense of confidence. Safe solo travel in grizzly country develops only through time, attention, and experience with all three working together. Situational awareness is the foundation of everything.

My approach to hiking protocol has developed somewhat differently from the guidance offered by some agencies. Much of the advice about bears, particularly in Yellowstone, centers on a single, easily communicated message: make noise. That guidance has practical strengths. It is simple to explain, straightforward to apply, and provides consistent direction for a wide range of visitors. In a park that receives millions of people each year, many with limited experience judging terrain, wind, visibility, or bear behavior, clear and broadly applicable guidance feels logical. Quiet travel, by contrast, depends on a person's ability to read what the land and animals are communicating and to respond in real time, skills that develop only through experience. Because that level of experience cannot be assumed, agencies naturally emphasize consistency, and guidance is often evaluated by whether it was clearly communicated and followed, rather than by how closely it matched the conditions of a particular situation.

Research on bear encounters often centers on the most dangerous scenarios, particularly surprise encounters at close range. These situations understandably shape much of the guidance around noise. At the same time, understanding how encounters develop can add important context. Sudden or loud human presence can alter the dynamics of an encounter, sometimes prompting stress responses from bears that are reflected in close-range incident reports.

I have found that noise does not function the same way in all contexts. In groups of three or more, noise can be useful, as a group presents a different profile to a bear. That same logic does not always apply when hiking alone. A loud, solitary presence can startle or unsettle a bear without the deterrent effect a group provides, and in some situations that reaction may increase risk, particularly when cubs are present.

Noise also has implications for disturbance in wild places. In core bear habitat, loud human movement can influence how animals behave. Feeding and movement patterns may shift, and in some cases bears move away from areas they would otherwise use. While this may reduce risk for people, it also affects the wildlife that live there, a balance that is not always visible.

Noise also affects the experience of others who come to wild places hoping to observe animals behaving naturally. When loud human presence dominates an area, wildlife may withdraw, routines can be altered, and the sense of being in a living, undisturbed place begins to fade. What remains feels less like a natural setting and more like one shaped primarily by human noise and movement.

The idea of making noise can be viewed alongside the original purpose Yellowstone was set aside to serve. The park was created to preserve natural conditions and to allow people to experience a landscape shaped primarily by its own forces, rather than by constant human disruption. Quiet, attentive travel aligns closely with that intent, as it relies on awareness rather than control. When guidance or practice leads to widespread disturbance, the experience can drift away from that purpose, with the landscape gradually shaped more by human presence than by its own patterns.

There are limits to what broad guidance can convey. Agencies communicate with a wide and varied audience, and their messaging cannot account for individual levels of experience. As a result, guidance tends to remain generalized, even though careful travel in wild places often depends on situational judgment.

A Note on Perspective

This chapter and this book as a whole reflect my own experiences and how I move through the backcountry. What is described here is simply what has worked for me over many years spent in grizzly country. Season, terrain, weather, and animal behavior all change, and judgment in wild places develops over time through attention and honest self-assessment. An approach that works well in one situation may not translate directly to another.

Responsibility in the wilderness always rests with the individual. Any choices made in response to what is shared here belong to the individual, shaped by personal ability, experience, and understanding of risk. This book offers my way of thinking and moving through wild places, not a guarantee of safety.

A Note on Off-Trail Hiking

Off-trail hiking is allowed in Yellowstone, but it comes with important restrictions. Some areas close unexpectedly. Bear

Management Areas close on set schedules. The park may also close trails for specific reasons. When I have doubts about where hiking is legal, I stop by the ranger desk at an information center and ask. Illegal hiking in Yellowstone National Park is a serious matter.

The Gear I Carry

My gear reflects self-reliance, not excess. I carry an inReach satellite communicator, a compass, a first-aid kit, fire-starting materials, and a poncho. I carry two cans of bear spray, one immediately accessible and the other in my pack in case the first is ever used. I have never had to use bear spray on any animal. I also carry a pocket knife, water, food, and mosquito protection. For observation and documentation, I carry a monocular, a Canon SX70HS, and a GoPro camera. Everything I carry has a purpose.

The Wilderness Humbles Me

It was the morning before I began a backpacking trip in Glacier National Park. I had arrived long before sunrise, while the world was still dark and quiet. I can't remember the exact trailhead now, but I hiked only about one mile to a small lake, a place easy enough to reach while carrying the heavy 4x5 large-format camera, tripod, and film gear I used back then.

Photography was serious for me. After being discharged from the military, I had built my own darkroom at home. I wanted to be a landscape photographer like Ansel Adams. I had studied everything I could about the Zone System that Adams developed, and I was ready to start applying it. Every photograph was a deliberate act. I had to think through each composition and wait for the right light while working out the exposure in my head. When the moment came, I would load a single sheet of film and take the picture. That slow, careful process kept me out there longer than most people, and over time it taught me to pay attention to light, to weather, and to the quiet details that shape a place. Photography became more than a craft. It was a way of learning the wilderness. Only later did I realize the real lesson wasn't just about photography, but about slowing down enough to notice the world around me.

I reached the lake before dawn and set up beside a narrow spur trail about 50 feet from the main path. The lake was still and perfect, as if it had been holding its breath through the night. A thin mist hovered just above the surface, drifting in slow, delicate swirls that barely disturbed the reflections beneath it. Snowcapped peaks rose beyond the lake, their shapes faint at first in the dim light. As the sky brightened, those same peaks sharpened into view, their reflections settling across the water with a quiet steadiness that felt almost unreal in the early morning calm. The air was cold, each breath waking me a little more to the stillness around the lake. I stood there quietly, listening to the soft sounds of the morning, the distant call of a lone bird and the faint creak of trees. Then the first light touched the ridges and a pale gold began to slide down the mountainsides. The bright sunlight on the peaks, contrasted with the shadowed lake below, pushed my skills to the limit. Calculations filled my head as I adjusted my lens and rechecked my settings. I wanted to catch that exact moment, doing everything possible to be ready for the perfect exposure.

Then something broke my concentration.

Everything around the lake had been quiet, and then suddenly there was a sound out of place. At first it was almost nothing, just a faint, muffled sound somewhere behind me. It came from the direction of the main trail. It was a slow, brushing sound, not like someone walking along the trail early in the morning.

I stopped what I was doing and listened. It was just getting light, still before sunrise, and I did not expect anyone else to be out here. The sound came again, closer now. I could feel the tension and unease rising in my body. Something was moving in the darkness of the trees. Whatever it was, it had to be some kind of large animal.

Then the sound became clearer. I could make out what sounded like footsteps now.

I turned and saw something large and dark brown moving through the dim light. At first I thought it was a horse, maybe an early rider. But the animal stopped, then turned down the same narrow trail toward me. It kept coming, slow and steady. I remember sitting there with a strange mix of curiosity and uncertainty, not sure whether to move or stay still. The animal came closer and closer until it stopped right beside me.

It wasn't a horse. It was a massive moose.

I was sitting on the ground, and the animal towered above me, so close I could have reached out and touched its leg without even stretching. It never noticed me. It stood still, facing the lake, staring out over the same view I had been admiring. For several long seconds neither of us moved. My mind felt blank, as if everything had paused at once. I remember thinking, "What am I supposed to do now?"

It felt like 15 seconds, though it could have been less. When a moose is standing within arm's reach, even a few seconds can feel like a lifetime. Finally, I decided to make a slow, gentle motion, just enough to let it know I was there. I raised my right arm slightly.

The moose caught the movement and exploded into action. It leapt straight out into the lake, splashing water high into the air. Then it circled about 25 yards out, turned down the shoreline, and disappeared into the trees.

When the sound of the splashing water faded, I sat there in the stillness, my heart racing. It was over as quickly as it had begun, and what a way to start a Glacier trip. That was the closest I've ever been to a moose, and I still can't believe it walked right down that trail, stopped beside me, and never saw me sitting there.

The moose encounter should have reminded me how small I was out there, but I brushed it off and kept chasing the idea of adventure. It was 1981, and I was fresh out of the Marine Corps, full of energy, confidence, and the belief that I could handle anything the wilderness threw at me. I didn't realize yet that the real lesson was still waiting for me up a backcountry trail.

Back then, backcountry camping in Glacier required a permit, and some camps had bear-proof enclosures, steel cages backpackers could sleep inside for protection. But that wasn't for me at the time. I didn't have the money for a permit, and I certainly wasn't going to spend the night in a cage. I figured I'd just hike in, find a quiet spot, and sleep under the stars, pretty much ignoring all the usual warnings for people with little experience in grizzly country.

A bit overconfident, the next morning I started up a trail under a clear sky, late enough that the light was already spilling through the trees. The air was cool, the forest quiet, and the ground damp with dew. Glacier's backcountry is a place of deep greens and tall lodgepole pines, giving way to open meadows and berry thickets glowing red and purple in late summer along the trails.

It was late August or early September, a time when the huckleberries were ripe. Grizzlies love berries. I knew that, but I wasn't thinking much about it as I hiked. I had never seen a grizzly in the wild and didn't expect to. But I would soon learn that this was prime grizzly territory.

About four miles up the trail, it happened.

Without warning, a large grizzly bear stepped out of the brush just ahead of me. It turned its head slightly and began walking up the trail slowly, almost as if it were ignoring me.

In those days, nobody carried bear spray as it hadn't been invented yet. I didn't have a gun either, and wouldn't have wanted one. I'd done my share of hunting when I was young, but now, killing an animal was the last thing I wanted to do. The only weapon I had was my Marine Corps K-bar knife, which wasn't much use in a situation like this.

So I just stood there, frozen.

Then another bear stepped out from the same spot. A grizzly, about the same size as the first, turned and followed the other bear up the trail. It seemed not to notice me.

I was still trying to process what I was seeing when a third bear stepped into view. This one was much larger. The first two, I realized, were likely older cubs, maybe 2 or 3 years old. This was their mother. The sow turned her head toward me as if to say a calm "Good morning," then turned up the trail to follow her cubs.

All three bears were now on the trail ahead of me, moving steadily away. None of them seemed alarmed. It was as if their focus was elsewhere, and calm avoidance was the unspoken rule.

They walked up the trail about 50 yards and disappeared over a small rise. I stood there for 30 seconds or more, the forest utterly silent around me. I wasn't afraid, just amazed at the sheer presence of these animals. Then I took a few slow steps forward, thinking maybe I would continue on. But after about ten paces, what I'd just seen hit me, how close they'd been, and how easily that situation could have turned. This was a grizzly family that I knew I needed to respect.

That was close. Too close.

That initial lack of fear was interesting. It was as if pure disbelief stepped in first, keeping the panic from rising. I didn't feel afraid for another minute or two. My mind was still processing what had just happened. But when the realization hit, it hit hard. That was dangerous, too dangerous.

I turned and started back down the trail. For a while I walked slowly, looking back more than once. Then my pace quickened to a fast walk, then faster. The feeling stayed with me all the way to the trailhead, that mix of alertness and the uneasy thought that the grizzlies might still be somewhere behind me, along with the relief that comes after a close encounter.

That night I didn't camp in the backcountry. Instead, I parked in the lot of a big hotel in Glacier and slept in the back of my CJ-5 Jeep. So much for the tough Marine who thought he could camp anywhere. Nature had taught me a lesson right there.

The next day, I did a couple of short hikes, keeping close to the road. The mountains were as beautiful as ever, but something in me had shifted. I had come to Glacier for adventure, and I found it, but I also found respect.

The bears weren't angry or aggressive. They were simply bears, moving through their home as they had for generations. I was the intruder, a visitor with a pack, a camera, and still a lot to learn. Yet I felt the grizzly mother had shown me respect, something I would always return in the years that followed, as I spent more time in their home.

That first grizzly encounter changed the way I saw the wild. It reminded me that I'm not in control out there. The wilderness moves on its own terms, where beauty and danger belong to the same world. I learned to stay quiet and to carry respect for wildlife in their home, and that lesson has stayed with me to this day.

Glacier National Park, September 1981

I Will Make My Stand Here

In early June 2013, I hiked the Bighorn Pass Trail, starting at the Indian Creek Campground on the Mammoth side of Yellowstone, off of Highway 89. The trail crosses the Gallatin Range and ends at the Bighorn Trailhead on Highway 191, about 22 to 24 miles, with roughly 2,500 feet of elevation gain. It's a full-day, point-to-point hike and one I had to plan carefully before starting.

I chose to hike this route east to west, from Highway 89 toward Highway 191, because Indian Creek has to be forded and, in early summer, the flow can be too high for a safe crossing. If I started from the west and found the creek impassable, I could end up stranded and in need of rescue. My wife dropped me off at the east Bighorn Pass trailhead at Indian Creek Campground and waited in Mammoth until I gave the signal for her to drive around to the other side of the park.

I carry an inReach satellite communicator whenever I hike alone in grizzly country. It allows my wife to see my position in real time and allows us to message each other while I hike. Solo hiking out here without a way to communicate isn't an option. This device could save my life if I were injured, attacked, or stranded.

I started before dawn. The trail begins on the south side of the Indian Creek Campground and runs along its edge for a bit. I always smile during that part because I've already been up for hours, driven over 100 miles, and now I'm walking quietly past tents where people are still snoring. Zero activity. If a grizzly walked through there in the night, and they do, most campers would never know it.

The first three miles of the Bighorn Trail in early morning are always a gift, with elk scattered through the meadows and sage, bulls growing velvet antlers, coyotes calling, sometimes wolves, sometimes a bear out in the open. The first light is soft, with color building in the east. The grass is that lush June green, growing fast under the warmth of spring. Behind it all, snowcapped mountains rise, the ones I still have to cross. That's what I love about doing a hike like this for the first time. I don't know what lies ahead, what obstacles I'll face, or what wildlife I'll see. I don't know if I'll meet grizzlies. I don't even know if I can do it. That unknown adds energy. That's life to me, exploring.

A little over two miles in, I crossed Indian Creek without trouble. It was as pure and clear as creek water gets. I felt a little guilty about stirring up the mud with each step as I crossed it. On the other side, I sent a message to my wife letting her know I'd made it across and that she could head for the west side. My best guess was that I'd reach her in 13 hours. The only question left was the pass itself. In June, snow often lingers heavy on top, and I wouldn't know if it was passable until I got there. The Yellowstone trail report said "impassable," but I knew no ranger had actually been up here. Yellowstone's trail reports are written for a broad range of visitors, many with limited backcountry experience, and they err on the side of caution, and I respect that. But it also means I won't really know until I get there.

About five or six miles in, the trail began to tell its story. Grizzly tracks appeared, plenty of them. Not fresh, but clear enough to bring my senses alive. The mud had dried around them, leaving perfect impressions. Prints on top of prints. A lot of coming and going. Tracks always look larger in mud because the foot spreads, pushing the edges outward. A six-inch print in mud might belong to a five-inch foot. However the prints were measured, there were plenty of bears around.

That realization always brings the backcountry to life. My pace slowed. Every sound, every scent mattered. I moved like a deer, a few steps, stop, look, listen. Then a few more. The forest was quiet except for birdsongs.

About a mile before the pass, I looked up the slope to my right and saw two black bears heading uphill, a male and a female, likely a mating pair. I zoomed in with my camera as they climbed away. It is unusual to see black bears moving that way, that fast, on such steep ground, like they were headed somewhere with purpose. Then, out of the corner of my eye, I caught movement to my right. I pulled back from the camera and saw a grizzly walking across a small opening about 30 yards away.

I trained the camera on the grizzly, thinking how great this was. Three bears already, this was a good day. Then, at that moment, I saw another flicker of movement. I looked, and it was another grizzly, a bigger one, apparently a male following the female. June is mating season, and that explained why the first grizzly was moving so fast. She was probably annoyed by the male constantly following her.

It started to sink in that I was standing near two grizzlies, ten miles from the nearest road. My camera began to shake, and I tried to steady it but couldn't.

The two grizzlies disappeared into the trees ahead of me, the same direction I needed to go. I had to decide whether to go forward or turn back. I was leaning toward turning around. It was already getting a little tense. Trees with small openings all around, two grizzlies close by, I half expected more to step out at any moment. Then the two grizzlies reappeared, walking back past me in the opposite direction. I was really starting to worry. I thought, "They don't know I'm here." But I was standing out in the open. What if they came closer? I remember feeling my body shake and forcing it to stop by focusing my mind. All I could do was stand there. They walked past, heading the other way, until they disappeared into the timber behind me.

That decided it for me. I would go forward. I started moving quickly to put distance between us. But about 100 yards later, they came back again from behind, moving through the same area, 35 yards away. Now I was really worried. I decided to yell, to make sure they knew I was there. This was the only time in my life I ever yelled at grizzlies.

I called out, loud and sharp, "Go away. Go away. Hey." The sound of my own voice breaking the silence sent chills through me. It scared me, not the bears. The female never looked my way. She just kept walking. The male glanced over at me as if to say, "I know you're there. I just don't care."

The grizzlies ignored me and disappeared into the trees again. I felt a little better. It was clear they had known I was there all along. What amazing animals. Here's little old me, and they could kill me in an instant, yet they let me be in their world. I felt bad for yelling at them. My fear began to fade, replaced by a sense of awe. Again the pair turned back, passed me one last time, and vanished behind me. I never saw them again. The feeling is hard to explain. It moves from fear to awe, and I wondered how many people in the world have experienced something like that.

I kept going. If they showed up again, I would stop and do nothing to disturb them. I didn't know it yet, but things were about to get much more intense. The snow deepened as I got closer to the pass, drifts, then bare trail, then drifts again. The trail cut through timber and brush, and the snow there was deeper than it looked. I stepped forward, broke through the crust, and dropped to my waist, stuck. I tried to dig out but couldn't get leverage. To my right was a rocky ledge, maybe 20 feet high, that offered a way over the drift. I was studying it when I heard something on the other side of the brush, coming toward me. Slow, steady breathing.

I froze.

The sound grew closer, deep, rhythmic breaths. There was no mistaking that sound. A grizzly was moving toward the thicket where I was stuck.

I became aware of only two things, the silence and the breathing of the bear as it drew near. My legs were pinned in the snow, but my mind was clear. I pulled my bear spray and held it ready. I couldn't see the bear through the branches, but I could hear it there, moving in that unseen space beside me.

A dozen thoughts passed through my mind in an instant, warnings I'd heard about hiking alone, stories of attacks and maulings. Then those thoughts faded away. I had to deal with what was next to me. What replaced them wasn't fear exactly, but stillness, as if every part of me had turned outward and was waiting. I remember thinking, I will make my stand right here. I also remember thinking this must be what it feels like when you realize how little control you really have, and that now, whatever happens, happens.

The breathing was close now, too close. Then a thought came, say something. Then, in a low, calm voice, I said, "Hey, bear. Go away, bear. Go away."

Silence. Instant, complete silence. The bear was gone. I never heard it turn or move. I stood there a long time, watching every direction, wondering if it was circling. Nothing.

When the adrenaline finally eased, I started digging out. I crawled to the base of the rock, stowed my spray, and climbed up. Topping out on that little cliff brought a sense of relief. From there I could see everything, snowfields, the pass, open ground, the canyon below. For the first time, I felt safe again.

Then I looked ahead toward the pass, and what did I see? Another grizzly. My sixth bear of the day, all within about 30 minutes. This grizzly was climbing straight up through the snow, pulling with its front legs and kicking with its hind legs, like a breaststroke in slow motion. And it was going exactly where I needed to go to cross over the pass.

I thought it through. I'd already seen two black bears, the mating pair of grizzlies that crossed in front of me three times, the bear that walked right up to me in the brush, and now this sixth one heading for the pass. I decided I would rather deal with the one ahead than all the bears behind. Still, it left me uneasy, another grizzly after everything else I'd already encountered. I was exhausted and didn't even bother with the camera. I'd seen enough bears for one day. I just wanted to get to a safe place.

I stayed high on the south-facing slope, where the ground was drier than the trail below. Patches of open earth connected between snowfields, and I followed them as far as I could. Then I came to a steep snowfield, at least 100 yards across. No way around it. I kicked footholds, one after another, steady and slow. Each move sent snow rolling away beneath me. One slip would have meant a long, steep slide to the bottom. But I kept steady and made it through. There was no going back.

Relief hit when I stepped onto the top of the pass, solid ground and open views. From there I could look west into the Gallatin Canyon country and back east toward Indian Creek and Yellowstone's interior. Everything below was opening up, meadows, scattered timber, green grass everywhere. I scanned for the grizzly that had gone over before me but saw no sign of it.

The country beyond the pass was beautiful and open. It felt good to walk on dry ground again, to have space around me, to see far. The rest of the miles were quiet and mostly downhill, giving me time to think.

It's hard to describe the mix of emotions after something like that, fear, yes, but also wonder and a sense of amazement. I replayed it. I asked myself what I could have done differently.

Then I realized there's a point where I did all I could do. I was there. I experienced it. I survived it. I learned from it. That's why I always say experience matters. I wouldn't tell anyone to go looking for a situation like that, but adventure isn't something that can be fully planned. It happens. It teaches.

I thought about the bears too. Even the one that came right up to me in the thicket seemed respectful once it knew I was human. The mating pair wasn't interested in me at all; they were focused on each other. The grizzly going up and over the pass might have been the same one that had been next to me in the brush. I don't know. But what I saw in all of them was this: when I stayed quiet and kept myself calm and respectful, they let me pass through their world and showed me that same respect.

The rest of the hike was uneventful except for a few miles of downed timber after the pass, just the usual stepping over and detouring around. No more bears, though I stayed alert. After a day like that, I did not stop paying attention.

I sent an inReach message to my wife when I was at the top of the pass. Later, she told me she really thought that was going to be the end of me.

Every hike teaches something, and this one reminded me how grizzlies react, how calm matters, and how traveling respectfully through wild country makes me a part of it, not a disruption to it.

I've always felt a connection with wildlife, but that day deepened it. Out here, with grizzlies, wind, snow, and miles of country, I feel more alive. The backcountry is beautiful in every way. I love being part of it.

— Yellowstone National Park, June 8, 2013

The Shimmering Bear
A Lesson in Readiness

I was already on the trail before sunrise, moving quietly through the timber. The ground was damp, soft enough to muffle each step. Everything was quiet, eerily quiet, except for the occasional brush of my sleeve or the faint sound of my pack shifting as I moved. Then, from somewhere in the dark timber to my right, a Great Horned Owl called out: a deep, resonant hoot that seemed to hang in the air. There's something haunting about hearing an owl in thick forest when everything else is silent. The sound echoes in a way that almost feels alive. I can't describe it properly but standing there, hearing it, and feeling it is amazing.

A few minutes later, as the trail curved through a darkened stretch of forest, I caught sight of something on the ground that stopped me in my tracks: grizzly prints. Big, clean, and fresh. I can tell instantly when tracks are fresh. These weren't weathered or faded; they still held the crisp edges of the bear's pads. The animal's heavy paws had lifted off the damp top layer of dirt, exposing the dry earth beneath. To my eye, that was one of the clearest signs the prints were recent.

I crouched down and studied them. Then, like I always do, I pressed my boot down beside one of the prints to compare the soil's texture. The trail was firm, so the edges of the track were perfectly defined, almost photographic. I didn't need a ruler to know the front foot was about five inches wide, probably from an average-size male, maybe 400 pounds. There were no smaller prints around, which meant no cubs. Wolf tracks followed right behind the bear. Big prints: about four inches across. A wolf trailing a grizzly. I have seen this before.

Judging by the sharp edges and removal of the damp top layer on the trail, both sets of tracks were less than one hour old. I remember standing there, just taking it in: the evidence of two powerful predators, both likely still somewhere ahead of me in the trees. It didn't feel like fear. It was more like being wide awake to everything around me. My senses sharpened.

It's fair to ask why I didn't turn around right then. But honestly, I see grizzly tracks on most of my hikes. Many of them are fresh, and most of the time, I never actually see the bear. Turning around would have gone against the reason I come out here in the first place, to feel the wild as it truly is, unchanged and alive.

The eastern sky began to glow as I moved farther up the trail. A thin line of gold spread across the mountaintops, and soon the sunlight was spilling over the peaks, catching the dew on the grass and the dark needles of the pines. That contrast of the warm light meeting the cool shadows always heightens my awareness of the beauty in the landscape. The air held that high-country crispness that comes only at sunrise.

I started to feel the warmth building, so I looked around for a good spot to stop and peel off a few layers. My eyes landed on a big pine beside the trail, with a nice open patch of ground beneath it and tall brush just beyond, a good place for a quick stop.

I knelt down, took off my pack, and set it beside me. It felt good to get off my feet. As I unzipped the pack and began stuffing my coat inside, something caught my eye: just a flicker of reddish-brown in the brush next to me. I froze, staring. At first, it didn't register. Then my brain caught up.

Bear.

It was enormous, and close. Too close. Maybe 12 feet away, half-hidden behind the brush, its massive head down, nose

30

buried in the dirt. It was digging for something, like grizzlies always seem to be doing: roots, a squirrel cache, who knows. The rhythmic sound of it pawing and sniffing somehow made it even more real. Instinctively, my hand went straight for my belt, reaching for my bear spray. It wasn't there. A sudden wave of alarm ran through me. I had taken it off earlier, and now my fingers scrambled to find it. I found it fast, but fast isn't the same as ready. For half a second, I thought about my camera, about filming what might have been one of the best encounters I'd ever had. But that thought vanished just as fast as it came. Filming could wait. Safety came first.

I lifted my eyes again, and the bear was no longer behind the brush. It had stepped out, onto the trail itself. The bear was turned sideways, the massive, broad-shouldered body gleamed in the sunlight. It hadn't noticed me yet. I was in the shadows beneath the pine, only 12 feet away, staring at one of the most powerful animals on earth, completely unarmed except for my bear spray and my voice.

I don't think I was even breathing. My thoughts narrowed to a single question: "What's the right move?"

I kept my voice low but firm. "Hey, Bear," I said. Calm. Controlled. My voice sounded steadier than I felt.

My voice startled me as much as the bear. The grizzly let out a deep, guttural grunt that I felt vibrate through my chest. Then, with a quick, powerful surge, it turned and thundered away. There was no aggression in its movement, just surprise and self-preservation. It wanted no part of me. In an instant, the calm forest erupted with motion. The bear broke through a dried-down tree, snapping brittle limbs as it passed, then ran along the edge of the lodgepole pines with astonishing speed. People say a grizzly can outrun a horse; watching this one, I believed it. It never slowed, never looked back. I watched it cover nearly 50 yards before it turned into the trees and dropped over the bank, disappearing as quickly as it had appeared. I stood there, perfectly still. The whole encounter had lasted maybe ten seconds, but it felt much longer. I was stunned with awe more than anything. That bear had been so close, so alive in the morning light, its coat shimmering with shades of brown and silver. It was one of those rare moments that stays in memory in a lasting way.

It took a while for my pulse to slow. Then, as the adrenaline began to fade, the reality became clear. I looked down at my bear spray and saw the safety clip still locked in place. That realization added a sobering layer to an unforgettable experience.

If that bear had decided to charge or even step toward me, I wouldn't have had time to do a thing. The distance was too close. The whole situation could have gone bad in an instant.

I sat down for a moment as calm slowly returned, along with a clear sense of relief that the bear had chosen the right direction to run. That encounter reminded me how fine the line can be out there, and how one small lapse on my part can change everything.

That's the thing about being in grizzly country alone. I can never let my guard down, not for a moment. I had become too comfortable when I stopped beneath that tree. I should've scanned the area more carefully before setting down my pack. Out there, complacency is the one thing I can't afford.

That morning left me with a few hard lessons of my own:

First, I was reminded how quickly my vigilance can slip when I get comfortable. Staying quiet helps me when trying to see wildlife, but it also means having to be twice as alert. I let my guard drop when I found that nice shady spot, but I got lucky.

Second, bear spray only helps if it's ready. Knowing where it is and keeping it within reach isn't optional. I realized how easily I could have lost precious seconds fumbling for it.

And finally, preparedness means practice. Having the spray is one thing, but remembering to pop that safety clip off when I need it in the wild; that's the part that sticks with me afterward.

As I packed up and continued on the trail, the morning sun had fully broken over the peaks. The forest looked different now, brighter, calmer, but somehow more alive. I didn't see that grizzly again, but I didn't need to. The memory of that shimmering bear, standing in the golden light just a dozen feet away, has stayed with me ever since.

It wasn't captured on camera, but it was recorded somewhere far better, in memory. And that's a moment I'll never forget.

Yellowstone ecosystem, August 2, 2015

When the Wild Reminds Me

It was a 3-day backpacking trip into the Lizard Lake country in mid-May. The morning was cold, 27 degrees, and the ground was still frozen from the night before. I crossed the Taylor Fork River on the footbridge and started up the trail just as the sun broke over the ridges. A low layer of fog hung just above head level. I could see clearly below it for some distance, but not above it. The grass and sagebrush were white with frost. Only a couple hundred yards in, I saw perfect grizzly tracks pressed into the frozen mud, along with marks where the bear had slipped and slid on the muddy trail. At first glance, the tracks could have suggested a huge grizzly. Although tracks often look bigger in mud, each print was about the size of a dinner plate. The sight encouraged me. It felt like a good sign to start the day. I had been up here a few times before, but had never seen a grizzly. I figured my chances were not great, though that thought was already starting to feel wrong.

About one mile up the trail, I stepped into a thick patch of willows growing along the creek to look at some tracks. I should have known better than to feel too comfortable walking through there. As I stepped out of the willows, a grizzly walked out of that same patch, only ten yards ahead of me. I froze, completely surprised, and slowly reached for my bear spray. The bear kept moving ahead and mostly to my left, never looking in my direction. She walked calmly through the sagebrush as if I wasn't even there. I eased my bear spray back into its holster and lifted my camera instead.

She stopped and looked uphill in the direction I was heading. I could clearly see the long, dish-shaped nose, the short forward ears, and the shoulder hump. She stood there gazing for 30 seconds, never turning toward me. My hands were shaking so badly that the footage turned out almost unwatchable. Then, from the corner of my eye, another grizzly appeared. This one was a huge, black-colored male, right in front of me, no more than 20 yards away. I still had the camera running. Like the first bear, he never looked my way, walking straight over the sagebrush instead of around it. His shoulder hump was massive.

He paused now and then to graze, head down, moving with that slow confidence grizzlies have.

All I could think about was creating space. I waited until it felt possible to move. When the male was about 50 yards off but still in plain sight, I began easing back as steadily as I could. I hoped the movement would not draw his attention. I backed up roughly 25 yards until only my head was visible above a small rise. I felt a little safer, but another worry settled in: they would catch my scent next. With both bears so close, I felt completely helpless. My whole body was shaking as I wondered what would happen when they realized I was there.

It seemed that neither bear ever saw me. After a couple of minutes, they drifted off into the trees. It was the beginning of mating season so this was a mating pair. The black male was one I recognized because I had been seeing him for years.

Encounters like this, when grizzlies act as if I'm not even there, have happened to me more times than I can count. It's how it goes more often than not. How can that be? Those moments have shaped how I move and behave in grizzly country and have taught me to stay quiet, respectful, and calm in their home. But in any case, the bears have to know I am there, especially at that distance.

After a few minutes, I collected myself and seriously considered ending the backpacking trip, heading back to the trailhead, and going home. I had done that on other trips when something like this had happened. But this was supposed to be a

3-day trip, so I told myself to stay the course. This was the kind of experience I had come for. How much better could a trip start out? I took a few deep breaths, gathered myself, and continued up the trail. Unknown to me then, in about 15 minutes things would get intense again.

Half a mile later, I looked back and saw another grizzly coming right up my tracks. This was a third grizzly. It was walking steadily, covering ground fast, and moving with purpose. I was not sure if it was following my scent or just heading the same way, but it was closing the distance.

I was beside a small lake, maybe 30 yards wide and 100 yards long. I figured my best chance was to cross it and climb the hill on the far side, where I could watch the bear from above. The edges were frozen, but the lake itself was open. Even though the air was below freezing, I did not think twice about crossing. I could see myself maybe having to swim. I waded in. Fortunately, the water only came up to my knees, soaking my boots and pants, but all I cared about was putting some distance between me and that bear and getting to a safer spot.

On the far side, I climbed to the top of a ridge and looked back. Nothing. The bear had vanished. That is the strange thing about grizzlies. One moment they are there and the next they are gone. I hiked to another ridge about 300 yards away and stayed there for a while, scanning with my scope. I knew that losing sight of the grizzly was not a good thing, but I had no choice. I had to keep moving and not waste any time doing it. I sat down, took off my boots, and changed into dry wool socks. My feet were cold, but I felt a lot better. I was really winded at this point, so I was relieved the grizzly never came into view again and that it was not following me after all.

From there, I continued off-trail toward the basin that leads to Albino Lake. Snow lingered in patches, soft and thinning as the temperature climbed into a gentle spring day. A small group of elk stood along the creek ahead, watching quietly before easing back into the timber. After passing the lake and hiking another mile and a half, I entered the place I have come to call the Grizzly Corridor. I have always found tracks there but never the bears themselves. Once again I found fresh prints in the snow, and these were traveling the opposite direction. If I had arrived an hour earlier, I may have met another grizzly coming straight toward me.

I knelt to study the tracks, noting the size and the distance between the hind foot and the front foot. That spacing helps me understand how fast a bear is moving. This one, likely an average female grizzly, was in a slow amble, making its way down toward the open area by Albino Lake. A short distance ahead, I stopped at a rubbing tree where grizzlies have worn the bark smooth throughout the years. The ground showed the place where they plant their feet and press their shoulders and back against the trunk. Tracks covered the snow in every direction. There was no mistaking the amount of grizzly activity in this place.

Beyond that point, the trail climbed through a few switchbacks before leveling out, with snow still covering much of the ground but easy enough to walk. By late morning it was warming quickly and the remaining snow was melting fast. As I reached higher elevation, the snowpack grew too deep to continue, so I turned back and walked about half a mile to an open area surrounded by trees. There I found a clear spring with cold water bubbling straight from the ground. It is hard to find anything that tastes better than water like that.

Later that afternoon, I set up my hammock with the front of the rain fly propped open so I could watch the night through my thermal scope if I woke up. Then I built a small fire, cooked a meal, and drank a cup of hot chocolate as the light faded. I settled into the hammock knowing grizzlies were moving somewhere in the darkness around camp. The problem I always seem to have is that I sleep so well, I never hear a thing. When I finally wake up and take a look, I see nothing at all.

The next morning I got up early, made a small fire to warm up, and watched elk grazing peacefully on a nearby hillside as I ate breakfast. I backtracked 4.5 miles and then took another trail toward Lizard Lake. I tried again to reach Lizard Lake but turned back when the snow grew too deep. I spent most of the day exploring and looking for wildlife. I saw plenty of elk and, far off, a view of Albino Lake below. By late afternoon along that trail I found an open spot with a good view, and it felt like the right place to camp. I was ready to call it a day. I set up my hammock where thick brush and timber formed a natural wall behind me. In front of me was open country and a short stretch of trail about ten yards away. It was a beautiful place to settle in. I cooked a hot meal and hung my food about 25 yards away, high in a tree, doing what I could to keep it out of easy reach of bears.

As evening settled in, I walked the area for a while and found fresh grizzly digs in the open ground but no tracks on the trail. It seemed the bears were working the thawed patches for roots and ground squirrels rather than traveling the path. Just before dark, I climbed into my hammock, ready for the night. Not long after the light faded, rain began to fall, steady and peaceful. There is nothing quite like lying warm in a hammock, listening to raindrops hit the tarp, and feeling dry and sheltered for the night. I slept soundly until morning.

As always, I was up before sunrise on the third morning. I can never seem to sleep once the sky starts to lighten. I woke to a beautiful view of the snowy mountains, with clouds and fog settled deep in the valleys. The sun was on the mountain peaks, casting that bright pink light that reflects off the snow and down across the top of the cloud layer below.

I packed slowly, hoping the fog that had drifted in around my camp would lift, but it stayed put. I set out anyway, walking straight into the heavy gray. By about nine o'clock, the fog was so thick I could not see anything without help. I had my thermal scope with me, and I relied on it as I moved through the Grizzly Corridor. Without it, I could only see a few yards ahead. I stopped several times just to listen. Even with the thermal, it is unsettling to move through thick fog in a place where I know grizzlies are close by.

Thirty minutes later, the fog finally began to thin, and I felt myself relax as I could see a little farther ahead again.

A mile from the trailhead I reached the same area where I had seen the first two grizzlies and where the third had come up the trail behind me. I was walking without much caution, already thinking about food and the drive home. Then I heard splashing, heavy and fast. I looked to my left. In the creek, only 20 yards away, were three grizzlies: a sow and two cubs, probably two years old. The cubs were about two-thirds the size of their mother, and one of them was a very blond color. I had not seen that before.

They had heard me first and climbed about 30 yards up the hill beside the creek before stopping. The mother stood in the center with the two cubs sitting on either side of her, all three looking straight at me. We watched each other for more than a minute, none of us moving. The cubs gave a few soft, high-pitched grunts, curious and unsure. They sat just like their mother, studying me. I stood quietly, watching them with my video camera running. I never felt any need to reach for my bear spray.

It is hard to describe a moment like that: a wild mother grizzly and her cubs, calm and unafraid, simply observing. The mother looked back and forth as if thinking, "I cannot believe you caught us off guard like this." The cubs seemed more curious than alarmed. After a while, the sow turned, gathered the cubs, and led them up the hill until they disappeared into the trees. The whole encounter lasted maybe 3 minutes, but it is one I will never forget.

By the time I reached the trailhead, I had seen six grizzlies on one backpacking trip, far more than I ever expected. The weather had been good, the nights down around 20 degrees, and the days in the 40s and 50s. It turned out to be one of my favorite trips.

The funny thing is, when I hike or backpack, it is always when I least expect to see bears that I end up seeing them. I do not know why that is, but it happens all the time. Maybe, the wild knows how to remind me to stay alert, humble, and thankful.

Taylor Fork, Yellowstone ecosystem, May 2017

A Lesson I Won't Forget
The Teepee Creek Encounter

I set out for a day hike up Teepee Creek, just outside the northwest corner of Yellowstone National Park. The country was soaked from the previous night's rain. Old tracks had been washed away, so any bear signs I found that morning would be fresh. One of the reasons I start out early is because I want to spot fresh tracks before they are destroyed by foot or horse traffic. For my part, I do the best I can to avoid stepping on tracks so they are left for the next person who might notice them.

Fog hung in the drainages and as it settled into the low places, softened the contours of the land. Even so, I spotted a bear roughly one mile away, a small dark shape moving through an open meadow. I raised my monocular and confirmed it was a grizzly. The bear was out in the open, digging and grazing in the fresh spring grass. From that distance, everything felt manageable. I could see the animal clearly, and it appeared at ease and unhurried.

I continued hiking for another half mile until a small hill came between me and the grizzly. If I stayed on the trail, I would no longer be able to see the grizzly. A band of fog hung just above the crest, drifting perhaps a hundred feet higher than the top. From below it looked thin and harmless, nothing more than a layer brushing the upper slopes, so I climbed toward the hill to gain a better vantage point for filming. The idea felt reasonable at the time. The bear was out of sight, the terrain looked straightforward, and the fog seemed high enough to remain above me.

As soon as I reached the crest, the fog moved in.

It thickened quickly and settled around me until everything vanished into gray. I stopped and scanned in every direction, but there was nothing to see. The world had closed down to a few yards. It was then that unease set in, not panic, just the quiet realization that a grizzly was somewhere close, possibly just below me, now hidden entirely within the fog. Grizzlies can move far faster than expected, and they can change position without making a sound.

Climbing up there had been a mistake. At that point in my experience, I was still willing to move closer to bears for the sake of better footage if I thought it was safe. I wanted to share what I saw, and that desire sometimes outweighed good judgment. That morning on Teepee Creek was the last time I ever made that choice.

I moved another hundred feet into the fog, and then it happened. A grizzly appeared 30 feet ahead, its massive shape emerging suddenly from the gray. Its head was down, grazing or digging, unaware of my presence. The distance was close enough to demand an immediate response. I stepped back, turned, and hurried down the damp hillside without running. As I moved away, I glanced over my shoulder, watching for any sign of reaction. There was none. The bear never saw me, never heard me, and never caught my scent.

Once I had put enough distance between us, I climbed a hillside roughly 300 yards away and positioned my camera near a climbable tree. The fog was still thick enough that I could not see the hill where the encounter had taken place, but I waited, hoping the bear would reappear.

As the fog slowly began to lift, a large buck rounded a corner below me, stopped abruptly upon seeing me, then bolted back the way it had come. I assumed the grizzly had pushed the deer in my direction while moving around the back side of the hill.

Because of that assumption, I failed to scan the thinning fog directly in front of me. Only later, while reviewing the footage, did I realize the grizzly had been on that slope the entire time.

Eventually the hillside came fully into view, and I spotted the bear again. It was on the same slope where I had first seen it, now about 200 yards away. That alone was a relief. As I watched it graze, another grizzly stepped into view beside it. There were two bears.

That realization changed everything. June is prime mating season, and during that time grizzlies often stay close together, sometimes only 15 to 20 yards apart. When I had walked into the fog earlier, I had not been 30 feet from a single bear. I had been close to two. One had been in front of me, and the other had remained hidden in the fog. I could have walked between them. The second bear could have been beside me or behind me without my knowledge.

Nothing escalated, and I think the fog muted sound. There was no wind. Neither bear saw me, heard me, or smelled me. At 30 feet, they had not detected me. That encounter taught me something important and specific. Grizzlies do not always pick up human scent at close range, depending on conditions. I have seen that confirmed many times since.

I remained on the opposite hillside, watching as the bears continued to graze calmly. The fog lifted completely, and I settled into a low spot where only my head and camera were visible above a small rise. The bears never noticed me. After getting some footage, I worked my way back down toward the trail, keeping my attention on the surrounding terrain. When I looked back, the two grizzlies were still behind me, grazing and slowly moving higher up the trail.

I continued down the trail and then cut south toward the Yellowstone boundary about a half mile away. I scanned the hillside to my left. The two grizzlies were still visible and remained unaware of my presence. Eventually the wind shifted. One bear caught my scent, stood abruptly, and bolted uphill. About thirty seconds later the second bear did the same. They never saw me, but once they smelled me, they left.

I do not like disturbing bears. It is better when they never know I am there at all. But once they caught my scent, they moved off, and I never saw them again.

The hike continued. The fog lowered again, then lifted. Light rain passed through, and I put on my poncho and kept moving. When the fog finally cleared, the country opened into bright green hills with low clouds settling into the valleys. A grouse appeared along the way, moving with that slow, deliberate walk they use when they believe they are unseen. I took a video as it worked its way through the brush.

Farther up, the views widened, and I began seeing fresh grizzly sign again. Tracks and digs were scattered across the slopes, likely left by the same two bears. That kind of sign always tells me bears are close, whether I see them or not. Being bear aware means reading those signs and staying alert to what they indicate.

At the Yellowstone boundary, I could look back down into Teepee Creek and across into Daly Creek. Fresh grizzly signs continued along the slope, grass laid over in long paths and new digs cut into the hillsides. This was clearly active grizzly country.

Down on the main trail, a group of tourists rode past on horseback. A few minutes after the riders disappeared, two black bears stepped out near the trail where the horses had just passed. The bears had waited quietly in the timber until the noise faded, then eased out into the open.

Out here, long strings of horses are common, but walkers are rare. Most people no longer move through this country on foot. Inside the park, they ride horses. Outside the park, they rely on machines. Walking, as a way of traveling through land, has nearly disappeared. Yet it is at a slower pace, one step at a time, that the land reveals what would otherwise remain unseen.

I stopped for lunch at a high overlook. While eating, I spotted two more black bears in the distance, feeding through openings before slipping back into the timber. It is remarkable how easily animals remain unseen.

Rain returned on the walk back to the trailhead.

This day on Teepee Creek and Daly Creek stayed with me. It was the last time I ever moved closer to bears for a better video. From that point on, I made a personal rule for myself that I would not approach bears. I choose to keep distance, leave the animals undisturbed, and accept what the zoom lens can capture.

Teepee Creek, Yellowstone June 2017

The Bigfoot Behind Me

Teepee Basin is a wild, remote corner just outside Yellowstone's western boundary. I had been there before, but this trip felt different. I planned to spend two nights in the high country, far beyond the reach of roads, lights, or voices.

Two days earlier I attempted this backpacking trip but turned around when there was a grizzly bear about a hundred yards ahead on the trail near the trailhead. I went home and decided to try again later.

I returned to the Bacon Rind Trailhead around 4:30 A.M. It was still dark. My awareness was already sharpened by the memory of the grizzly I'd seen here two days earlier. The stars

51

were out, and the eastern sky held the faint glow of approaching dawn.

I didn't use a headlamp, yet I could still see my breath as I moved slowly, watching the ground ahead. The only sounds were the crunch of my boots on the trail and the steady trickle of the creek. When it's dark, I usually move about 100 feet, then stop, look, and listen. I scan for any moving black shape, knowing it is either a bear or a moose.

For the first couple of miles, the path followed the creek through timber, the air rich with the smell of lodgepole pine. At a familiar bend in the canyon, I left the trail and began climbing toward Teepee Basin. This is where the hike truly begins. It is steep, rugged, and off-trail, exactly as I prefer.

There's a feeling that comes with going off-trail that's hard to describe. Every step becomes a decision: picking a line through deadfall, weaving between trees and rock slides, and watching for scat, prints, or a dark shape moving in the timber. I had been up this way several times and had never seen another person. Bears, yes. I encountered plenty of them, but never people.

As I climbed, the wilderness began to wake up. First the birds, then the light. The ridges turned gold, and the meadows glistened with dew. I stopped a few times to catch my breath and look back over the valley. In that vastness, I felt a quiet freedom. I was the only one there, free to wander wherever I chose and camp wherever the view felt right.

It was late July, and before leaving I hadn't given the mosquitoes much thought. However, I am always prepared. I carry repellent and a head net, and as it happened, I required both.

In one swampy stretch, the swarm grew so thick I could hear the buzzing from a distance. I put on my head net and applied repellent, rubbing it over my hands, neck, and face. I avoid aerosols, which stink and spread scent everywhere. Mosquitoes are relentless by day, but when the sun drops and the air cools, they vanish as if someone had flipped a switch.

By late morning, I was about six miles in, high on a ridge that led into the basin. I decided to stop for a break and a cup of hot chocolate. I found a familiar clearing, a perfect opening that looked out over the surrounding mountains and valleys.

I dropped my pack, set my tripod and camera a few feet away, and sat on a log to enjoy my hot chocolate. The air was still. Not a sound. No birds, no wind, just the heavy mountain silence. I remember thinking how peaceful it felt.

Out of habit, I glanced behind me, something I always do when I stop. This time, something was there.

At first glance, it looked like Bigfoot. That is no exaggeration. A huge, upright figure stood on two legs, half-hidden by timber, pushing a small pine as if to attract my attention. The tree was maybe 5 inches thick and 15 feet tall, swaying like a sapling in the wind. Perhaps a sound made me turn. I don't remember.

For three or four seconds, I sat frozen, watching it move the tree. It was close, no more than 20 yards away. The swishing sound was rhythmic, and my mind could not make sense of what I was seeing.

Then instinct kicked in. I needed a video. I stood, grabbed my camera, and swung it toward the trees, but the figure had vanished. Just like that.

The forest had taken it as if it had never been there.

I stood with the camera ready, waiting for movement. Nothing. Silence returned. That's when it hit me, what I might have just missed. If I'd hit record a few seconds sooner, it could have been one of the best wildlife videos I'd ever captured. Maybe one of the best anyone ever had.

But here's the thing. I don't believe in Bigfoot. I'm sure it wasn't that. It must have been a grizzly or a black bear standing upright, looking straight at me. I remember a round face with small ears and dark eyes. It appeared to be a cross between a grizzly and Bigfoot. My drawing at the start of this chapter is a close illustration of what I thought I saw.

Still, my mind can play tricks. When I only get a few seconds of something wild, my mind fills in the blanks. One moment I see a bear. The next, something almost human-shaped. Memory shifts in strange ways.

I walked to the spot where it had stood. The ground was soft and springy, thick with years of accumulated pine needles. It was the kind of surface that holds no tracks. I searched anyway, circling the area for a print or any signs. Nothing.

After a few minutes, I stood still and listened. Every sense was on high alert, my camera ready. But the woods were empty. Whatever it was had moved on.

I hiked on, still thinking about it. Every time I turned a corner or crossed a clearing, I glanced over my shoulder. After such an event, awareness sharpens. Every shadow looks alive.

That night, I set up camp higher in the basin. As I pitched my tent, I couldn't stop thinking about that moment, how close it had been, how strange it felt. I wondered if it might come back. Solo camping in grizzly country forces the imagination to run wild.

Once inside my sleeping bag, the world grew calm. I slept well. There were no sounds or visits; at least, there were none I detected. Only a steady breeze stirred the pines, followed by a short rain shower.

The next morning, I woke to the sunrise spilling through the tent. The ridges glowed orange. I sipped hot chocolate, thinking about the day before. Never before had I turned to find something standing there, staring right at me. For a split second, it looked like Bigfoot pushing and swaying a tree back and forth.

I laughed, shaking my head. It's funny how fast your mind jumps to the wildest possibilities when you're caught off guard.

But I'll admit, part of me was disappointed. That could have been one of the best videos I'd ever captured. One of the best encounters. I still wish I had caught it on film. I wanted the evidence to show others and the clarity to confirm what I witnessed. However, as I would later discover, technical failures would have made that impossible regardless.

I've thought about that moment a lot since. What kind of behavior was that? I've watched grizzlies dig for roots, rip apart stumps, roll rocks, even scratch their backs on trees, but never push a tree like that. Was it a territorial display, play, or mere curiosity? I do not know.

Encounters like that remind me that no matter how well I know these animals, they are still capable of the unpredictable. There is always a level of mystery that remains. I have had numerous bear encounters before and since, but that one stands apart. It was not my closest or most dangerous encounter, but it was undoubtedly the strangest. One second I was sipping hot chocolate in peace, and the next, I was face to face with something that challenges memory itself.

Two days later, while descending the mountain, a second bear encounter revealed a frustrating truth about the footage I had missed. I was deep in the timber and exhausted from three days of camping. Because I was focused primarily on my footing, I failed to notice my surroundings as clearly as I should have. My mosquito net obscured my vision. Wearing it in bear country was a dangerous compromise; while it stopped the mosquitoes from eating me alive, it also blurred my surroundings.

Then came the unmistakable sound of a bear charging. It was the rhythm of a steam locomotive; air forced out with each stride, punctuated by grunts. No other sound compares. The sound originated directly ahead. Through the mesh of my net, I saw a large black bear emerge from the timber. It executed a bluff charge and stopped 30 yards away, visibly agitated.

I grabbed my camera, a Canon SX50 on a small tripod and flipped it on, aimed, and hit record.

Flash.

An error message.

The bear stood perfectly framed. The screen read: "MEMORY CARD ERROR."

I knew the fix, and I knew it was painfully slow. I had to unscrew the camera, open the plastic door, reseat the SD card, and remount the device. By the time the camera was ready, the bear had turned and walked back into the timber.

I stood there, frustrated by yet another missed opportunity.

Twenty yards later, thunder. The bear charged again, closing the distance. I raised the camera and hit record. The same error appeared.

"Are you kidding me?" I said through the net. I power-cycled the camera, off, on, record. It ran for maybe three seconds before freezing again. Just enough to catch a flicker as the bear disappeared. I couldn't believe it. I had never had camera problems before.

Then came the final blow: a sharp crack of branches to my side and a loud "woof." The bear had circled and charged from the flank. I spun, and raised my camera. The bear stopped just barely in sight, then slowly backed off into the trees.

I hit record again. This time the device functioned, capturing five seconds of footage as the bear retreated. Five seconds; that was the extent of my documentation after three bluff charges.

The walk back to the trailhead was long and silent. I replayed the trip in my mind: the tree-pushing Bigfoot bear, the black bear's bluff charges, two of the best wildlife opportunities I'd ever had, and both videos were lost.

The irony was cruel: had I tried to record the first bear, the same memory card error would have ruined the footage. It was two strikes of bad luck. Nevertheless, I realized the moment was not lost. I had been fully present for the experience, even if the camera had not.

One thing stood out as I thought about it. I never once reached for my bear spray. I was so focused on the camera, on trying to understand what I was seeing, that the thought never crossed my mind. That surprised me later, when I thought about it. In the moment, I felt no fear. I was tuned into the situation, not alarmed. Somehow, I knew the black bear's charges were bluffs. I can't fully explain it, but I never felt in danger.

I learned a difficult lesson: always verify equipment before departure. I had purchased a high-capacity memory card incompatible with the Canon SX50. I never repeated that error. I may not always be fast enough to record every moment; however, since thenI have never lost footage to a faulty card since. That trip proved that while preparation can fail, the wilderness never does. The bears were magnificent. The mystery, the unpredictability, and the raw wildness are what keeps me coming back. Regardless of how often I believe I have seen it all, nature always finds a way to surprise me.

July 2017, Yellowstone ecosystem

The Night at Shelf Lake
When the Dark Played Tricks

The day began with a stop at the Visitor Center in West Yellowstone to get a backcountry permit for campsite WE5 at Shelf Lake. The office opened at 8:00 A.M. and when I pulled into town a little before seven, all was quiet. Most tourists seemed to start their days late. I had already been up for three hours and had driven a 100 miles, yet it felt like the town was just waking. I hoped to start up the Specimen Creek trail by nine or nine thirty, which would put me at the lake by midafternoon.

If a permit wasn't available, I planned to hike past the lake to the Sky Rim Trail and camp just outside the park boundary.

The drive from West Yellowstone to the Specimen Creek trailhead is about 30 miles. Mid-September in this part of the country usually brings a stretch of weather with temperatures in the mid-sixties, no mosquitoes, and far fewer visitors. It's the best time of year for this kind of trip. I planned to be out for three days and two nights with the second day spent higher along the Sky Rim Trail exploring the tops of the Gallatin Range.

The trail to Shelf Lake in Yellowstone climbs more than 2,000 feet over about nine miles, ending high in the Gallatin Range about 9,200 feet. It's the kind of hike where I might see mountain goats, bighorn sheep, black bears, or grizzlies. Much of the way is thick with pine, the kind of timber that closes in tight and limits what I can see. In country like this, spotting a bear with my eyes is unlikely. For me, what matters most is knowing how to read the signs they leave behind: tracks pressed into the trail, overturned rocks, pressed-down grass trails through the brush, fresh scat. I have always felt that without that kind of attention to detail, I could walk right past a bear without knowing it.

About four miles up the trail, I heard movement off to my left through the trees. Morning hikes are usually quiet with only the sounds of nature. There are no aircraft overhead, no distant engines, nothing man-made. Because of that, any sound that breaks the stillness is worth listening to. This sound had a rhythm I couldn't place, steady but not moving away, and that made me curious. I dropped my pack beside the trail, made sure I had my bear spray, and stepped quietly into the timber. About 100 yards in, I found the source: a young mountain sheep, a bighorn, trying to jump up to the same ledge where its mother was standing. The ledge was only about five feet high, but every time the little one reached it, there wasn't enough room for both, so it would jump back down. It kept trying until the mother finally moved to another ledge, and then the young sheep made it up on the ledge. I watched from the shadows about 20 yards away, and I don't think they knew I was there. Moments like that are part of what makes hiking so interesting. Out here, I never know what I'm going to see.

There are mountains and cliffs on both sides of this stretch of the Specimen Creek trail all the way up to the junction for Crescent Lake and Shelf Lake. About five miles in, I passed a backcountry campsite with tents still zipped and no one stirring. It always amazes me how people sleep through the best part of the day. Morning is when the air is still, the light is clean, and the animals are moving. Just above that campsite, high on the cliffs, stood a small group of mountain goats which the sleeping campers would not see. I wonder why people come this far only to miss moments like these. I stopped to watch the goats for a while. The trip was off to a good start. Most times when I hike Specimen Creek, I see signs of wildlife but rarely the animals themselves.

The last three miles from the junction to the lake told me I was walking in bear country. The trail steepened sharply there, a long, hard climb with a heavy pack, and every step took focus. Fresh black bear tracks were imprinted across the dirt, scattered like quiet warnings. With each print, I felt as if I could see a bear at any moment, but the strain of the climb kept my attention narrower than it should have been. I didn't see any grizzly sign that day, and maybe that absence made me less alert than I normally am. This is good country for both species, yet all I saw were tracks from black bears. By the time I reached the lake, I had already stepped past more prints than I could count.

Shelf Lake rests in a steep-walled cirque, a small glacial basin where winter snow gathers and melts slowly through summer. The lake is a glacier-created tarn with no visible inlet stream and no outlet. It's fed almost entirely by snowmelt and a little rain, with any outflow likely sinking into the ground and wandering downslope out of sight toward the Specimen Creek drainage. Yet the lake always seems to have plenty of water. Normally, I wouldn't draw drinking water from a lake with no inflow or outflow, but here it's the only source, which makes me think it may also be fed by an underground spring. Pines ring the shore, cliffs rise behind it, and the place feels completely backcountry, cut off from the world.

After dropping my pack at the campsite on the bank above the water, I took a moment to let the stillness settle in. The only sound was a breeze brushing through the pines, and because this was September, there were no mosquitoes. That matters more to me than I used to realize. Nothing can ruin a long hike faster than fighting mosquitoes from morning to night, and the freedom from them made the whole place feel even more peaceful. As I stood there, I thought about the bears that lived in this country. Knowing that grizzlies and black bears are around is everything to me. I can't imagine backcountry camping without them. Without bears, a place like this would feel empty, almost dull, as if the edge had been taken off the experience. The real adventure comes from sharing the mountains with something wild, something that requires me to stay aware and honest with myself. Being perfectly safe has never held much interest for me. I come out here to experience the real thing, to test myself a little, to see how I handle it. To me, grizzly country is the only place that I feel is worth camping.

I set up camp, boiled a quick meal, and with daylight still left, started up the slope toward the Sky Rim Trail. The path climbed through scattered trees and open grass, and even there, high above the lake, I kept finding more bear tracks on the trail. It was clear I was sharing the mountain that evening, and that added a quiet kind of excitement to the adventure. This was why I was here.

The night ahead would be moonless, complete darkness except for stars. I set my light and a can of bear spray beside my head and crawled into the tent. It's always surprising how a thin layer of fabric can make me feel sheltered. Inside, I feel like I'm out of the night's reach, even though it's only cloth between me and whatever moves out there. That small sense of enclosure brings enough comfort to let me relax.

This tent does have issues, though. Its shape narrows at the feet and opens near my head, which leaves me sleeping toward the widest and most exposed part of the shelter. I would rather rest with my head against something solid, a trunk or a boulder, anything that feels anchored. Instead my head ends up where a bear would most likely pass, and the thought is enough to keep me aware of every small sound.

My camp was about ten yards from the lake, but the water was so still it made no sound at all. I drifted off thinking about the quiet, the clean air, and how far this place felt from everything human.

Nights like this always begin with quietness. Once I'm in the tent, the stillness works on me, and I fall asleep without a trace of worry. Out here I usually sleep so deeply that nothing stirs me, not a sound, not a shift in the wind. Fear never finds me once I'm asleep. But this night would be different, not because I felt afraid, but because the noise outside would grow loud enough to disturb even my best sleep.

Somewhere around one in the morning, I woke to a sound. I wasn't sure if I'd heard it or dreamed it. Then, a little while later, I woke again to the sound of splashing. I lay there, trying to decide if this was a dream or the real thing. The splashing started as a faint stir, then grew into a racket of heavy water movement, unmistakably close. It sounded as if something large was right below my tent in the shallows.

I lay still, every sense awake, listening to the water move in steady bursts. Time slowed with each splash. I counted them without trying, one after another, each followed by a quiet so sharp I didn't dare move a muscle. What else could I do at that point? Before long, I convinced myself it had to be a bear. What else could make a noise like that? Bigfoot crossed my mind for half a second, but I don't believe in Bigfoot.

The sound came from no more than 30 yards away. The longer I listened, the more the darkness pressed in. I reached for my flashlight and aimed it toward the water. The beam caught only the nearest trees, and beyond them the light seemed to disappear. The lake stayed hidden. Whatever was out there kept splashing as if the light meant nothing, as if my presence there made no difference, and the realization left me uneasy in a way I had not foreseen. Something that close shouldn't have been so fearless.

I shut the light off and lay back down, wide awake, listening. 15 minutes passed. The steady noise of water and movement went on and on. My thoughts began to turn. What if it came up here, brushed against the tent, started sniffing around? When I set up camp earlier in the day, I had stacked some tree limbs around my tent for that very reason. If a bear came close, the sound of the limbs moving or breaking would wake me. My mind built every possibility the dark would allow. Finally, I decided to make a sound, just to let it know I was here. I said softly at first, "Hey, bear." Then louder, "Hey, bear!"

The lake went still. I heard the faint drip of water and, in my mind, could see the bear casually walking out of the lake. Then nothing. No footsteps. No breathing. Only silence. I lay there another 20 minutes before I even moved. In time, I drifted back into uneasy sleep, troubled by what I had done. The bear hadn't been bothering me; it was only playing in the water. I'd let fear take hold and chased away a creature that had simply been enjoying itself in its home.

At first light, I got up and went straight down to the shore. I expected to see tracks, but there were none. I walked the edge of the lake for about 25 yards in both directions. Still nothing. Then I followed the trail out of my campsite, the same one I'd brushed clear the evening before. About 35 yards from camp, fresh black bear prints appeared. I looked carefully. Nothing near my tent. It seemed the bear had come up the hill and stepped onto the trail right here. I followed the prints around to the far end of the lake, nearly 150 yards from camp. There the sand was full of signs: a pile of scat, and big, wet impressions leading in and out of the water. That's where the bear had been, not right below me as I'd thought. The sound had carried through the still night and made the bear seem almost beside me. What had felt like danger close by was far away.

That morning I sat by the water for a long time, thinking about how easily fear can twist what's real. If I'd stayed quiet, I might have learned something more about how bears play in the lake at night. Instead, I ended the moment before it could teach me anything.

Since then, I've tried not to chase away what I don't understand. The splash of water. The creak of trees. The sense of unseen company in the dark. It's all part of the wilderness, and it isn't meant to scare me. Sometimes it only asks that I listen and trust that not every sound is a threat. I'd already learned not to yell at bears, but that night the lesson came differently. It came in the dark, where quiet has its own way of teaching.

Ever since, my sleep in the backcountry has been great, as if the wild itself was keeping watch. The night out there is simple: wind in the trees, cold air, and a stillness that covers the lake. Even with bears close by, there's a peace that runs deeper than fear, and it feels like belonging.

Yellowstone National Park, September, 2017

A Quiet Standoff

Few people hike in the Thunderer area of northeast Yellowstone National Park because crossing Soda Butte Creek is difficult and the terrain is steep and demanding. This out-and-back hike covers ten miles, with roughly 2,500 feet of elevation gain. I have always been struck by how different this area feels from much of Yellowstone. Even in mid-summer, it remains lush and wet, with small creeks crossing the trail, moss and ferns growing thick, and the ground often soft underfoot.

I have only felt comfortable doing this hike after late July, because earlier in the season Soda Butte Creek can run too high.

I started early. It was not fully dark, but there was enough light to see clearly. Visibility is essential for crossing Soda Butte. That morning, I crossed without changing shoes, though I usually do. The ground here stays wet; once boots get soaked, they rarely dry.

After the crossing, the trail passes through open meadows before entering steep switchbacks leading toward Thunderer Mountain. Not long into the climb, I found large grizzly tracks pressed into the mud. The fresh, sharp tracks shifted my focus, and the effort of the climb faded, replaced by the realization that any encounter would be directly ahead. In that thick timber, I have often noticed bears moving along trails as the path of least resistance.

A short distance up the trail, I stopped where a large avalanche or snow slide had come through during the winter. I have snowshoed in this area before, and the scene reminded me that it is not a safe place to travel in winter. Trees lay snapped and twisted, their trunks pointing downhill. Despite the moisture, mosquitoes were surprisingly absent. Wildflowers were still blooming, and the area felt active and alive.

By the time I reached the saddle, which I think of as the top of the climb, I had gained just over 2,100 vertical feet. I did not plan to continue to the summit. From the saddle, I left the trail and headed east. Thunderer Mountain rose behind me to the west, while a series of open ridges and basins stretched out to the east. West of the saddle is better habitat for bighorn sheep and mountain goats. East is better bear country. I headed east.

The off-trail hiking was easy. There was little deadfall, the vegetation was lighter, and the ground was open and rocky. The views extended far in every direction. Before long, I began seeing more signs of grizzly activity. Several trees showed fresh scratch marks. Unlike tracks, scratch marks are harder to read. Some could have been made earlier that day, others perhaps days before. I moved slowly and deliberately, watching for any kind of movement. I was there to see bears, not to scare them.

After about a half mile, I decided to turn back because I had not seen anything, and it seemed like a good time to reverse direction. Before doing that, I found a small rocky opening and sat down to eat lunch.

While sitting there, I noticed movement in a cluster of saplings roughly 50 yards ahead. Two bears were making their way toward me from the same area I had just walked through less than 15 minutes earlier. At first glance, I assumed they were black bears. I started my video camera, stayed seated, and continued eating. As I watched more closely, it became clear they were grizzlies. They appeared to be subadults, roughly three-quarters the size of a full-grown adult. How close might their mother be? They may have been recently separated from their mother. There was no way to know for sure, but I remembered the fresh scratch marks high on the trees from earlier.

Given their size, I remained where I was, watching. Under normal circumstances, staying seated might not have been the best choice, but I felt comfortable remaining still. I sat on a narrow finger of land with steep slopes dropping away on three sides, leaving few options for a quiet retreat. More than that, curiosity outweighed fear. I wanted to observe their behavior and their reaction. Should they continue to approach, I wanted to see how long it took them to detect me. Though they were the size of adult black bears, my primary concern was a nearby mother.

As the bears closed the distance, they continued to graze. They ate constantly: stepping forward, reaching to one side, and biting off whatever greenery was within reach before shifting direction to repeat the cycle. They never remained stationary. They fed while moving, covering ground steadily and efficiently.

When they were about 30 yards away, a few flies began circling around me. My occasional efforts to brush them away caused small movements. One bear noticed.

That bear climbed onto a log and stood there, looking directly at me. Then it looked away, scanning the area in other directions. For a moment, it seemed undecided. I stayed still. The bear climbed down, moved a short distance, and then climbed onto another log. This time, it stood upright on its hind legs, facing me. Something changed. Its posture and expression reflected confusion and rising agitation.

The bear dropped slowly and remained on the log. Its nose lifted high and moved back and forth as it tested the air. Its ears were stiff and alert. Then it began clapping its jaws, a sharp, hollow sound that carried clearly. It did not sound aggressive. It sounded uncertain. After a few seconds, the bear turned, took several steps, and bolted with the distinct swish of a running grizzly.

The bear ran 25 yards, stopped in an opening, and turned. Instead of continuing on, it came closer again, closing the distance by roughly ten yards. It climbed onto another log and stood there, studying me. It clapped its jaws again, shook its head, and tested the air as if trying to understand something entirely unfamiliar.

The second bear had been closer all along. It remained in thick vegetation below my position, seemingly unaware of me. Dense brush likely blocked its view. Eventually, the bear emerged and moved toward the first. It seemed curious rather than unsettled, as if trying to understand the other bear's reaction. Both bears stood on separate logs, ten feet apart, facing me. Their ears were up, noses lifted, attention fixed. One appeared uneasy; the other simply watched.

After a while, they began moving away. Their posture reminded me of a cautious cat, backs slightly arched, heads low, glancing sideways while keeping me in view. They would move a short distance, stop, look back, graze briefly, then stop and stare again. Even as they worked their way out to nearly 100 yards, they kept checking behind them.

Eventually, they stopped grazing altogether and stood still, watching. I wondered what they were thinking in that moment. Throughout the encounter, I remained aware of the possibility that their mother could appear at any time.

The more agitated bear moved differently, walking along logs rather than through the grass. It would step onto a log, walk its length, jump down, then climb onto the next. Each time, it would stop, lower its head, turn sideways, and stare.

At last, both bears moved up and over a small rise roughly 200 yards away. Even then, they continued turning back every few seconds, repeating the pattern of moving, eating, stopping, and staring until they disappeared from view.

Since I was heading in the same direction, I waited where I was for about ten minutes before moving. When I eased up toward the crest of the rise, I saw them again, 50 or 60 yards ahead. One bear had found a dry log and was tearing it apart for ants. It was remarkable how easily it ripped layers of wood loose with its front claws. Within seconds, ants covered its legs and face. The bear lifted its feet, rubbed them together, rubbed its face, and even hopped briefly on one leg as it tried to lick ants off the log. After a moment, it jumped down, turned, and stared directly at me. It was clear both bears had been watching to see if I was still there.

After they moved on and were no longer visible, I waited another ten minutes before approaching the log. It was full of medium-sized ants. The bear had reached them quickly and efficiently.

I did not see the bears again. I assumed they had moved into thicker timber. I headed back down the ridge to rejoin the Thunderer Trail.

On the return, I passed a well-used rubbing tree and several others marked with deep claw gouges, some of them reaching eight feet up off the ground. Those marks were likely made by a much larger grizzly, possibly the mother.

It was rare to observe two subadult sibling grizzlies behaving naturally at close range without their mother present. Once they noticed me, curiosity held their attention far longer than I expected. One appeared uneasy, but neither approached. I remained seated and quiet. I was prepared to stand and use bear spray if necessary, but restraint on both sides prevented that moment from arriving. Instead, we studied one another, each trying to understand something unfamiliar.

Another lesson I have learned repeatedly is that just because I see no bears on the way in does not mean I will not see them on the way out. After hiking for hours with the hope of seeing wildlife, there are times when nothing appears and that hope quietly fades. When that happens, focus can slip. The pace quickens, the effort to move quietly eases, and attention shifts away from footing and surroundings. Caution gives way to routine, and that is when awareness matters most.

That day, curiosity outweighed fear, and restraint turned what could have been an ordinary hike into a rare and memorable encounter in Yellowstone's backcountry.

Thunderer Cutoff Trail, Yellowstone

July 30, 2019

Too Close
to Mother Grizzly

I started out early that July morning, the air a comfortable fifty degrees, as the sky began to lighten. July is one of the finest times to be in Yellowstone. The grass is a deep summer green, wildflowers brighten every slope, and the long stretch of daylight gives the feeling that the whole landscape is awake. Animals with their young move through the open country, and the valleys feel full and alive.

I always choose areas far from the places tourists visit, the quiet corners where the only sounds are wind, birds, and the soft movement of animals feeding. Most visitors arrive in loud groups, their voices carrying along trails and across open ground. I prefer the silence. It allows me to settle in, listen, and stay tuned to what is happening around me.

This time of year, anticipation comes easily. On June and July hikes, I almost always see bears. I never know where they will appear, but I feel that sense of nearness, as if one could step out of the grass at any moment. That awareness keeps me alert, and it draws on habits and instincts I have formed over many years of moving alone through places like this.

Not far up the trail, I saw a moose standing about 100 yards ahead, staring straight at me. I stopped and watched it for a while. It was a bull, growing new antlers that still looked small for the season. Moose rarely run from me. They tend to stand and watch, calm but curious, as if deciding what kind of presence I am. This one was no different. Its dark shape stood against pale sagebrush and new grass, its head turning slowly as it checked the surroundings. After a few moments, it went back to feeding.

I continued climbing through patches of new growth mixed with tall dried grass from the previous year. The sun had not reached the peaks yet, but the light was clear enough to see a long way. Elk grazed ahead, easy to pick out in the open. When sunlight finally spilled across the slopes, their coats lit up with rich color against the green hillsides. One elk stepped a little closer, curious and unhurried, then lost interest and drifted away. Scenes like that still stop me, even after seeing them many times.

Eventually I reached a ridge. I had seen grizzlies here often enough that I felt certain one would be nearby. Before easing over the top, I checked the wind. It was almost dead calm. I looked at the sun as well. Its position matters. This morning it was rising off to my left, not working against me.

I began lifting my head slowly over the ridge, letting the ground come into view inch by inch. As I rose higher, what had been hidden just beyond the crest gradually revealed itself. By the time only a narrow strip remained unseen, I treated every step as if something could be waiting just out of sight. If a bear appeared close, my plan was simple. Back away immediately, create space, and keep everything calm.

As soon as my head cleared the ridge, I saw a grizzly about 100 yards out, grazing in the flat below. It was a large blond bear with darker tones mixed in, feeding peacefully among sunflowers and wild geraniums. The air was still, and the bear had no idea I was there.

As I watched, the bear began drifting in my direction, not with any urgency, just following a steady line of feeding that gradually closed the distance. The space between us was shrinking. I prefer to observe bears without them ever knowing I am there, and this felt like the moment to protect that boundary. I started backing away before the distance tightened further.

Even as I moved off, the bear remained part of my awareness. I could no longer see it, but I stayed alert to where it might reappear. I turned down the trail, moving quickly but quietly, and glanced back often, watching the ridge and knowing the situation was still active behind me.

Less than 100 yards later, I saw movement in the sagebrush ahead. Grizzlies can be difficult to spot there, their bodies no taller than the brush when they are on all fours. I have learned to notice the dark line of shoulders and back sliding through pale vegetation. This time, that dark shape appeared suddenly and unmistakably. I froze. I knew immediately what it was.

I began easing away, not straight back, but at an angle. The first bear was still somewhere behind me, and I did not want to drift toward it. The bear ahead kept feeding with its head down, completely unaware that I had been only about 25 yards from it moments earlier. With bears now on both sides of me, I had to be very careful about how I moved.

At first, I wondered if they might be a mating pair. But it was mid-July, well past that season. What I was dealing with was two separate adult grizzlies using the same area at the same time. I had walked into the middle of it.

When I reached what felt like a safer distance, perhaps 100 yards, I paused and felt briefly in control. I made a poor decision then, one that has stayed with me. I set my tripod down and filmed myself easing away, thinking I would return for the camera afterward. It was a careless choice, driven by the urge to document the moment rather than leave it alone.

When I walked back and lifted the camera, I turned it toward the grizzly. In the viewfinder, two small shapes suddenly appeared beside her. Cubs. One close to her side, the other a little farther out, both partly hidden in the grass. It was the first time I realized she had young with her.

That changed everything.

Only minutes earlier, I had been inside the danger zone of a mother grizzly with two cubs, while another adult bear was still somewhere behind me. The place I had moved to turned out to be the right one. Being caught between two adult grizzlies can become dangerous quickly, especially with cubs involved.

As I filmed, the sense that I was managing the situation began to slip away. The mother caught my scent. She lifted her head, then rose onto her hind legs, testing the air. A mother grizzly standing like that is an unsettling sight. She was not threatening yet, but she was deciding what would happen next, and that decision was entirely hers.

Her ears were forward, her nose working. She looked straight toward me but did not notice me. I stayed completely still. She dropped back down, made a soft call, and both cubs ran to her, pressing against her hind legs. She turned and walked away at an angle, guiding them out of the area. She stayed calm, alert, and deliberate.

Once she began moving off, I stopped filming. I had already pushed things too far. I picked up my camera and moved in the opposite direction, checking behind me often, watching both where she went and where the other bear might appear. I kept moving until I felt I had put real distance between myself and all of them.

For the next mile, I eased along, stopping often to look and listen. I stayed out of the timber, leaving that dark cover undisturbed. Fresh grizzly tracks pressed deep into the grass told me bears were still nearby. Every time I come out here, I hope to see bears. I had seen plenty that morning and was ready for the rest of the hike to be uneventful. It had been enough.

After another hour of steady walking, I finally felt the tension ease. I saw a few deer on the way out, but my thoughts stayed with that encounter, with the mother and her cubs, and with the narrow margin I had walked without fully realizing it at the time.

It had only been a few hours, but the intensity had been enough for one day. When I see grizzlies ahead and I cannot see a safe way through, I always turn around. I have made it a personal rule not to slip past bears at close range, especially family groups.

Even so, the day remained beautiful. The light stayed low, shadows stretched across the hills, and sandhill cranes called from every direction. Moments like that are reminders of how wild and full of life this place still is. Moving through country like this, I feel the difference between merely existing and actually living.

Yellowstone ecosystem , July 18, 2021

The Quiet Balance
Between a Grizzly and Me

The hike began in darkness. I started up the Bighorn Trail at least half an hour before there was enough light to see the path clearly. It was June 1, and winter still held parts of the valley. Broad patches of snow one foot deep lay scattered between bare stretches of earth, so my steps weaved from dry ground to crusted white as I worked my way along the trail. This part of Yellowstone always carries an early presence of grizzlies and black bears along the creek, and I like to start before sunrise to catch a bit of that morning life. But doing so also means I might pass within yards of a bear in the dark without ever knowing it.

Over the years, I have seen enough night encounters to feel that grizzlies can behave much the same in darkness as they do in daylight. At night, their sight seems limited to me, but their hearing and sense of smell still feel sharp. If something makes a sound and they cannot see what it is, they sometimes move a little closer out of curiosity. But once they seem to register that I am human, they often turn away with the same steady manner I have seen in full sun.

In the gray light, the first shape I noticed was an elk. It stood quietly about 40 yards away, watching me for a moment before lowering its head to graze again. The stillness around it made the calls of Canada geese all the more striking. Their honks echoed across the frozen trail and the open flats. It was the time when their eggs should be hatching, the mothers settling their bodies over the new chicks to hold in the warmth.

As the sky brightened, the light became strong enough that the camera could record more easily, so I let it run while I walked. I did not know it then, but a male grizzly was moving somewhere nearby. Fresh signs are hard to notice when the ground is frozen, and I had seen none. The geese were easier to detect. Their calls rolled through the valley, a reminder of the wildness of this place.

Ducks shared the ponds with the geese, swimming calmly through the same waters. Neither species seemed to trouble the other. They drifted and fed side by side with a simple ease. A few geese rose on their legs and stretched their wings, slow flaps that looked like the first motions of the morning. It made me wonder again how they ever keep their nests safe at night from grizzlies.

I have never had an answer. My best guess is that their nesting sites are chosen carefully and defended hard. They place them in parts of these wetlands I would not want to walk into, and I imagine that is the whole point.

While I watched, five geese came flying low over the river, calling loudly as they landed near the bank. I wondered where they had come from and what drew them to this particular stretch of morning light. Everything around me felt alive and stirring.

A little farther on, a small pond lay perfectly still, the surface reflecting the sky like polished glass. A crow called somewhere in the trees, and its voice carried across the cold air. Sounds always seem to travel farther at this hour. Behind me, the mountains were catching the first strong sunlight. This was the kind of morning when everything in the valley seems to wake at once, including the geese, the ducks, the elk, even the small things moving along the banks. There is only a narrow window each season when all of this lines up so perfectly. A week earlier or later and much of this activity fades, shifts, or disappears altogether.

As I continued up the trail, the day opened around me. A soft light spread through the east. Mist curled above the creek. The peaks beyond the valley took on the first color of morning. The water beside the trail flowed smooth and clear, carrying reflections of the pink sky and the dark outline of the forest. It was one of those mornings that slows a person's steps.

Then suddenly a grizzly appeared, walking at a slow, unhurried pace along the trail toward me. The valley was open in this stretch and the river lay close beside the path, leaving little room for cover. It was a large bear, as any grizzly looks when a person is alone on the trail. I saw it at roughly 120 yards and stopped immediately, standing in the open while it came on with its head raised, looking calmly from side to side.

I didn't move. The grizzly didn't act as if it saw me. When it closed the gap to less than 100 yards, the moment tightened. It seemed ready to continue on and walk right past me, as if my presence didn't matter at all. I decided it was time to make sure it knew I was there. Turning and retreating across open ground would only draw more attention, and any quick movement felt wrong in a valley this wide and quiet. From experience on these trails, I've learned that staying calm is often the only real option, and that a bear needs the chance to recognize what stands ahead.

So I raised an arm and waved it slowly back and forth. The bear stopped, lifted its head high, and looked straight at me. It watched for maybe 30 seconds, not alarmed in the least at my presence, which was exactly what I had hoped for. Everything was quiet, the creek, the trees, the air itself. Once I knew it had seen me, I stopped waving and waited. It stood there, thinking in that way bears do when deciding their next move. Then, to my surprise, the grizzly chose to continue straight down the trail toward me. The way it moved felt almost courteous, as if it intended to pass politely and continue on its way.

That was worrisome. I stayed where I stood, trying to read its body language. When the grizzly reached about 80 yards, I waved my arms again, and it stopped once more. I decided I had better say something. It hardly matters what a person says, but I said in a calm voice, "Hey bear, hey bear." The grizzly did the same thing again, taking a long look and studying me for 15 seconds before deciding once more to continue toward me.

I will admit I was beginning to worry. I had not seen this kind of behavior before. The grizzly acted polite, but it was still a wild and deadly animal, and no matter how well I thought I was reading its body language, I could be wrong. It walked ten feet, stopped to look at me, then walked another ten feet and stopped again. It was clear the bear was trying to make its own decision, yet it kept coming. When it reached a distance that left me no room for error, I realized I had to move back and do it in a way that would not alarm the bear. The strange thing was that we both made our decisions at the same moment. The grizzly turned around, and I backed away and up the hillside about 100 yards.

It turned off the trail and headed toward the river. For a moment the bear looked as though it would cross and go around me. I was thinking, this is working out. The bear is going to go around at a safe distance and I will be able to continue on this hike.

But when it reached the water's edge, it paused, leaned out over the river to look across, and then turned back. It changed its mind about getting into the water.

As it walked along the bank, I couldn't help but notice the scene around it. The grizzly moved quietly beside the river, its dark coat standing out against the frost-covered grass. The bright sunlight was just beginning to reach the valley floor, touching the hillside behind it and brushing the grasses just beyond the bear with a warm, early light. For a moment it felt like the whole valley was holding still. It was just me and the grizzly in that open space, the sun spreading across the morning slopes, and the distant calls of geese carrying through the cold air. Even with everything uncertain, the scene was striking in its beauty, as if the land offered a brief pause before the next decision.

Instead of crossing the river, the grizzly angled in the other direction, cutting across in front of me, still more than 100 yards away. It began working its way up the hillside, the same hillside I was standing on, though a little higher.

When it reached the slope above me, it turned again, now moving in my direction along the tree line of the hillside, still at a safe distance but closer than I wanted it to pass. At that point I decided it was time to completely change my plans, stop hiking farther up Bighorn, and head back to the trailhead.

Back on the trail, I walked quickly to stay ahead of the grizzly. Experience has taught me that a grizzly's pace is always quicker than mine. Even when I couldn't see it, I had the sense it was gaining ground somewhere behind me in the trees. That feeling alone was enough to make me leave the trail and angle toward the river, putting more distance between myself and wherever the bear might be moving.

After about three-quarters of a mile, a small hill beside the river caught my eye. It was lit by the first strong sunlight of the morning, the whole slope washed in a warm glow. It looked like a good place to stop. When I stepped into that light, it felt like the tension of the last few minutes eased, and there was a sense of relief in finally moving out of the shadows and into the sun. After the darkness and the weight of the moment, that sunlight felt like a small refuge, or at least as close to one as the valley was going to offer.

I was thinking that if I could spot the grizzly moving along the trees on the far side of the trail, I might be able to let it pass at a safe distance and then work my way back up the trail. At this point, I was at least 200 yards from the trail, far enough that I had room to watch and make a careful decision.

While I watched for movement, something else caught my eye. Another grizzly was coming up the trail from the direction of the trailhead. At first I thought it might be the same bear, just farther ahead than I expected, but its direction told me otherwise. It was moving toward the spot where the first grizzly would be, and this one looked bigger. It walked straight up the trail at a faster pace, steady and deliberate. The thought struck me that if I had stayed on the trail instead of cutting toward the river, I would now be face to face with this grizzly, with another closing in behind me. It was a realization that sharpened the moment and made clear what I had just avoided.

Knowing there were now two bears heading toward one another changed everything. This would not stay a calm situation for long. If one startled the other, they could both bolt my way. At the very least, one might chase the other in my direction. I knew I had to move, and move quickly, keeping out of sight of both bears.

I started moving away calmly but at a quicker pace, working through the sagebrush as best I could. The brush was only hip high, yet thick enough that every step risked a stumble. After about 50 yards I looked back. The second grizzly had left the trail and was now angling in my direction. Seeing it leave the trail brought a sharper sense of urgency. I knew I had to get out of sight again and move fast, even though I was already getting winded from pushing through the sagebrush.

The only option was to drop back down toward the river. The tall river grass along parts of the bank would be easier to move through than the solid sagebrush, and it would keep me hidden from both bears. I slipped down to the river and followed the bank, staying out of sight. I moved quickly, watching the tops of the high banks and the small rises along the river in case one of the grizzlies came over. If that happened, I knew I would have to decide whether to swim the icy water or stand my ground in the open. Fortunately that choice never came. I went nearly a mile before climbing another small hill to look behind me. Both bears were gone and I couldn't see them anywhere.

Reviewing the video clips later gave me a chance to think more clearly about the morning. It was the middle of mating season, and the two bears were a male and a female, likely a pair that had become separated during the night. Each had been searching for the other, or perhaps closing the distance for the first time. The more I reflected on it, the more I saw that my alarm had been stronger than necessary. They were intent on finding each other, not creating the grizzly sandwich I thought I had avoided.

In my view, that also explained the behavior of the first grizzly, why it kept coming in my direction even with me standing there. It moved with an easy, steady manner because it was simply trying to get past me to reach the other bear. That morning reinforced my sense that those bears were intent on their own business, not on me. They would rather avoid me. I have never felt that humans are on their list of things to eat. Grizzlies carry a strong sense of self-preservation, and they instinctively know to stay clear of people when they can. Even in the middle of mating season, with its instinct pulling it toward the other bear, this grizzly did everything it could to go around me, to slip by without trouble, and continue on its way. Most of the time a bear is simply trying to move through its own country without conflict.

I also realized that while I had been hiking in complete darkness earlier that morning, the male grizzly was somewhere nearby. That part did not bother me much. I often start out in the dark, and from time to time I hear a grizzly bear, or something large, step off the trail ahead of me and move around me in the darkness. With more than 700 grizzlies in the Yellowstone ecosystem, they are always out there whether a person sees them or not. Most people never realize how close bears can be, even in broad daylight, moving quietly through the same country without ever being noticed.

It turns out I was simply a traveler passing through the middle of their story.

Yellowstone National Park, Bighorn Pass Trail, June 2022

A Hyperphagia Encounter
Grizzly Encounter During Hyperphagia

I start a little later than usual on this hike, waiting for enough light to clearly see where I am stepping. I normally begin long before sunrise, but this route is completely off trail and does not start at a trailhead, so beginning in daylight makes sense. The hike begins with a crossing of a creek and continues through an open, swampy field with narrow, deep holes, terrain that would be dangerous to cross in the dark. From there, the route climbs steeply over the first mountain before dropping slightly into excellent grizzly habitat where I have seen bears many times. This is the time of year when grizzly bears are in hyperphagia, the period when their bodies shift from building muscle to storing fat in preparation for winter hibernation.

As I climb, I notice that the grass and Arrowleaf Balsamroot sunflowers are dried out, making it impossible to move as quietly as I would like to. Still, the low morning sun at my back is warm, and the long shadows and golden light are striking. There is a quiet satisfaction in knowing I got up early and drove two hours to be here. This opening stretch of the hike alone feels worth the effort.

I move at my normal slow pace, maintaining a strong awareness of my surroundings. This area offers excellent bear habitat, with older grizzly digs scattered throughout. The terrain is a mix of clustered pine trees and small open grassy areas, ideal for grizzlies feeding on pocket gophers and underground bulbs.

Fall color is everywhere. I turn often to take in the views, noticing the bright yellow grass set against the dark pine trees and the distant mountain forest. A low, full moon sits to the west. The weather is perfect. All of it sends a quiet surge of energy through me, and anticipation builds for what I might see on this hike. This is the kind of place where the chance of encountering another person is nearly zero, but the chance of seeing a bear is great.

After crossing over the top, I head down into the first large opening. I have seen a lot of wildlife in this spot. I approach very quietly, fully alert, knowing there could be a grizzly in the open or just beyond the next tree or cluster of brush. I do not see anything at first as I step into the tall yellow grass, nearly three feet high. As I walk farther toward the middle of the field, the shape of something rises out of the grass. Near the trees, a black hump becomes barely visible.

A bear moves slowly and casually, drifting slightly in my direction. It lifts its head often to look around. I can see it scenting the air, its mouth slightly open. The hump is massive. As it closes some distance, I plan my next move. I want distance between us, and I want it without adding pressure to the moment. I ease backward in small increments, aware that any movement could change everything. The wind is in my favor, preventing the large male grizzly from detecting me by scent. The downside is that the bear remains unaware of me and continues drifting closer.

In close encounters, fear is not the first emotion I feel. Fear comes later, when there is time to replay it in my mind. In the moment, everything narrows to what needs to be done. I already know from past encounters that I must have my bear spray out, with the safety off. I like to stand my ground when necessary and back away slowly when I can. Most important, I need to work to keep the grizzly in a calm state.

It is extremely quiet here. For me, breaking that silence with my voice feels wrong. I worry that speaking could change the moment in ways I cannot predict. If I move very slowly, the grizzly may notice me while still settled, then move off on its own.

I am facing the grizzly. My breathing is steady, and I remain still, letting the moment unfold. At this point, the bear has not yet seen me.

The grizzly moves into shorter grass where I can see it clearly. It zigzags, stopping often to lift its nose high into the breeze drifting in my direction. The bear is very fat and appears to be wandering rather than actively feeding. It moves through good gopher habitat without digging. The bear is striking with its nose high in the air and turned away from me. Its broad shoulders, massive head, and forward-pointing ears are a powerful sight.

I am also thinking carefully about my bear spray. The wind is blowing from the bear toward me. A straight spray would come back into my face. If the bear closed the distance, I was thinking I would have to move to the side and spray at an angle.

Eventually I reach the edge of the field. The grizzly is back in the trees on the far side, about 40 yards away. That distance is still much closer than anyone ever wants to be to a grizzly. I can see it clearly now. It seems more interested in smelling the trees than feeding. It appears to be checking for the scent of other grizzlies, spending long moments with its nose pressed to the limbs of small trees.

Watching this bear, I begin to notice how often real encounters unfold differently than expected. The movement is unhurried. There is no obvious urgency, no intense focus on feeding, and no sense of pressure driving its behavior. It looks much like many other bears I have observed at different times of year, calm, deliberate, and attentive to its surroundings.

After a few minutes, the grizzly turns and begins walking toward me again, keeping to the tree line. It finally spots me and lifts its head high. The bear slows, turns slightly to one side, and continues on, hesitation visible in its movement. A few steps later it glances over again without fully turning, then reaches a small tree about six feet tall. Rising onto its hind legs, it swats the tree and drops back down. When it settles onto all fours, it faces me once more.

At that moment, I notice what looks like foam around the bear's mouth. It is subtle, but visible. Foam can form quickly when a bear is agitated, sometimes within a minute, yet only about ten seconds have passed since I thought the bear first saw me. I realize then that the bear had already known I was there. I have learned that sometimes, even when a bear seems unaware of me, it already knows I am present. That lesson stays with me whenever I am in grizzly country.

When eye contact happens, I do not look away. I never have with a grizzly. I think grizzlies have an automatic caution toward humans, and I do not want to weaken it by showing uncertainty. Looking away feels like something I cannot bring myself to do.

People often call the grizzly the apex predator, but that framing feels incomplete. Man is the apex predator. Holding that thought gives me a strange calm, even if it changes nothing.

The grizzly is showing no aggression. Still, it is becoming agitated. This is the moment when complete readiness matters. The grizzly knows I am there and has not moved off. It is still assessing the situation. Even though I believe I can read its behavior, I know I can be wrong. Bears can also change in an instant. My approach stays the same. If it comes too close, I will stand my ground and use the spray.

Then the grizzly sinks back into the darkness of the trees. I walk slowly in the other direction. A few minutes later I spot it again in roughly the same area, doing what it had been doing before, smelling trees.

It was a large grizzly, and it did not want me there, but the situation resolved without escalation. As with other encounters I have had during this time of year, nothing about this one felt unusual. The bear showed no interest in me beyond assessing the situation.

Watching the bear move off through the timber, the encounter settled into something familiar rather than exceptional. It fit a pattern I have seen many times before. Encounters like this often linger with me because they quietly challenge how hyperphagia is commonly described.

This bear behaved no differently than others I have encountered during August, September, and October in previous years. By moving through excellent feeding habitat without actively foraging or eating, it showed the opposite of what is often implied. The behavior I observed felt measured and consistent with what I see across seasons. Grizzlies can be protective of food sources at any time of year, but that defensiveness does not appear suddenly or universally in the fall.

Grizzlies eat according to what each season provides, and their feeding behavior is driven by food availability. When high-quality food is available, they eat heavily. When it is not, they do not. In winter, they do not eat at all. If rich food were abundant year-round, a grizzly would not suddenly eat more in September than in June. Feeding would simply continue as long as food remained available.

Scientists describe hormonal changes that increase appetite during this period, and I do not dispute that. What I do not consistently observe, however, is a visible change in behavior. What stands out instead is continuity. Outside of mating season, feeding dominates much of a grizzly's daily activity whenever food is present.

What is often interpreted as increased feeding in the fall appears, in practice, to reflect increased food availability. As the season changes, food becomes more concentrated. Berries ripen, agricultural crops become available in some areas, nuts and cones appear in certain regions, and late-season vegetation still holds moisture. When food is denser and easier to reach, bears naturally spend more visible time feeding. That does not necessarily mean their hunger has changed. It means the landscape has.

Hyperphagia is a biological state, not a conscious behavioral switch. It involves hormonal changes that prepare the body for winter and shift physiology toward fat storage. Those changes do not appear to cause a bear to eat more than it would if the same food were available at other times of year. If peak-season berries were available in April, June, or even December, a grizzly would feed in the same way.

This becomes easier to see in places where food is consistently abundant. On Kodiak Island, for example, bears do not always hibernate and often remain fat throughout the year. Their behavior does not shift sharply in the fall because food conditions remain stable. At places like the Grizzly and Wolf Center in West Yellowstone, bears are fed throughout the winter and do not hibernate. Their intake remains steady because their environment does. These situations offer a clear demonstration that what is often described as a fall feeding frenzy is closely tied to food concentration. Their physiology changes, but their decision-making and temperament remain consistent.

This is how I have come to understand grizzly feeding behavior through repeated encounters in the field. Grizzlies feed heavily whenever food is available, and the intensity of that feeding changes with food density. I have often heard people say that it is more dangerous to be in grizzly country at this time of year because bears are entering hyperphagia and are therefore more aggressive. That is not a direct quote, but it is the conclusion at which many people seem to arrive. From what I have seen, that explanation can oversimplify what is actually happening and, in some cases, needlessly alarm people.

Hunting season also overlaps this time of year, and many encounters between hunters and grizzlies occur then. Those encounters are sometimes attributed to hyperphagia, when in reality they may involve a bear responding to the presence of a carcass or another concentrated food source. I often see fresh grizzly tracks leading out of the park and into areas where elk and deer hunting is taking place. It suggests to me that grizzlies respond quickly to where food becomes available. What is often described as hyperphagia does not present itself in the field as a sudden shift in behavior. Feeding intensity follows food availability, not a conscious awareness of the coming winter or a deliberate change in temperament. From what I have seen, bears continue to feed where food is concentrated, and that can be misread as a change in behavior when it may not be.

October 2, 2023 Yellowstone ecosystem

The Moment That Changed
the Morning

For a moment, I sat in the car debating whether to wait for a little more light. June 19th seldom brings much of a dawn chorus to listen to. If any calls were going to break the quiet, they would come from coyotes or wolves, but with the car window down there was nothing to hear. Another thought nagging at me was the trail itself, which began in timber, and the fact that this country held a high concentration of grizzlies. That was the very reason I chose this place, although the thought of meeting a grizzly in the dark was not something I wanted. Eventually I stepped out and started up the trail in the darkness.

A couple of days earlier, I had hiked this same route with a friend. We had found plenty of grizzly evidence but never saw the bears that made it. I hoped to combine both days of footage into one video, and for that to work the sun needed to be in roughly the same position along the way.

Walking up the trail I could see well enough to avoid holes or rocks. My friend had used a light during our earlier hike, but I seldom use one. I prefer my eyes to adjust to whatever the morning gives me, just enough to keep from stumbling.

Hiking in darkness is a different kind of experience. In the wilderness the mind leans heavily on sight, but darkness shifts that balance and brings sound and smell to the forefront. The whole environment changes character. Movements feel slower, and every step settles into a quieter kind of awareness.

After so many years of hiking alone in grizzly country, the routine can grow familiar to the point where the sense of discovery begins to fade. I have seen hundreds of bears on foot and have walked through more close encounters than I can count. At times, it seems as if there is little left to surprise me.

Even so, those minutes before first light still hold something that keeps me coming back. I have never been able to wait in the car until the sun appears. Two decades ago, I often started early enough to travel several miles before the morning took shape. Slough Creek was one of those places. I once began at two in the morning and reached the four-mile mark by first light. The first stretch of that trail holds a heavy concentration of bears, and during one of those early starts, about three miles in, I ran straight into one. The bear jumped into a bush beside the trail and stayed there. I tried to film, but the viewfinder was nothing but black. I could barely make out its outline, and after a minute, it slipped back into the trees. Encounters like that were not rare. Running into a bear at night happened many times, each one reminding me how different the world feels before the light returns.

When I pass that spot now in daylight, it still amazes me that I once hiked that far in utter darkness. These days, I do not start that early because there is no opportunity to film, but I still like to begin before the morning arrives. The sounds and the experience feel different from any daytime hike. So, off I went into the dimness. This encounter would unfold differently from any other I had experienced in early-morning darkness.

After ten minutes or so, my eyes adjusted. I could pick out the dark outlines of trees and brush, studying them closely. If any shape shifted even slightly, that movement would likely belong to a moose or a grizzly. The sky was brightening enough that the silhouettes were clear. My thoughts turned to the timing. If all went well I would reach a place known for grizzlies just as the sun cast its first long morning shadows.

Then, a dark spot moved. Only a small shift, but unmistakable. It was on a low rise to my left, about 20 yards away. I stopped at once. As my eyes tried to focus, the shape resolved: a large grizzly facing slightly uphill. It seemed unaware of my presence, its nose down as if it were smelling the ground or feeding quietly.

I took a couple of steps back as the bear climbed toward the top of the rise. Against the lighter sky, I could finally take out the camera. I didn't try to focus, knowing that any attempt in that low light might ruin the chance of capturing even a fragment of the moment. Fortunately, the camera happened to be in acceptable focus already.

The grizzly moved among the scattered trees on top of the rise. Then everything shifted. Somehow it noticed me. I hadn't taken more than a breath, but the faint noise of the camera and the brush of my coat must have carried. It stood about 25 yards away, on the rise that curved around in front of me. The trail dipped before climbing toward that small hill. When it sensed me, it rose onto its hind legs and looked down in my direction. I kept filming, waiting for it to turn and leave, but it didn't. Instead it dropped back to all fours and began deliberately zigzagging down the slope toward me.

That kind of movement is unusual. I did not expect the grizzly to approach after detecting me. The situation shifted instantly into an emergency, and I turned and started down the trail. I rarely turn my back because it removes any chance to track a bear's intentions, but I had to move. My monocular fell out of its pouch. For an instant, I debated leaving it, but instinct made me pick it up and pull out the bear spray.

I took four or five more quick steps. By then the grizzly should have been right behind me. I turned with the safety off, ready.

Nothing. The trail was empty.

I listened hard. No branches, no huffing, no movement at all. The bear had vanished. My best explanation is that it approached just enough to catch my full scent and then changed direction at once. The last glimpse I had was of it coming downslope. After it disappeared into the small dip ahead, it simply never appeared again.

I hurried down the trail, glancing behind with nearly every step. Relief washed over me when the car came into view. The encounter had happened less than 400 yards from the trailhead, and it took only a few minutes to reach the car again.

Even with all the years spent in grizzly country, darkness can still reveal something new.

Yellowstone ecosystem, June 2025

What Goes Unseen

Over the years, I have walked past many bears before they were ever noticed. It is a pattern that has repeated itself across hundreds of hikes and many years. The question that keeps coming back is simple: How many bears have I passed at close range (less than 50 yards) and never seen, never even known they were there? I can't ask this question lightly or casually. I have to be truthful with myself about what I know from experience. Sometimes my wife, a friend, or another set of eyes behind me pointed it out. Other times, I turned around and saw what I had just passed. In either case, if the bear had not been noticed when it was, I would have kept walking right past.

As I examine the evidence, these truths become clear.

* A lot of bears are probably nearby without ever being noticed.

* I have found that my own calmness often shapes how I experience an encounter.

* In many moments, the bears have not acted as if I were a threat.

* At times, it seems as if animals pick up on something deeper than movement alone.

* Agitation has a way of spreading.

These points are not theory for me. They are built from moments on real trails, in daylight and darkness, in brush and open ground, with bears close enough to matter.

A bear can be close and still disappear into the terrain, especially if it is not moving. My eyes pass over it. The best evidence comes from the times a bear was noticed only after I had already passed it. Those moments are measurable in a simple way: the bear was close, and it was missed by me.

Another way I get my estimation is by watching other animals. For example: When I hike in winter and deep snow covers the ground, foxes suddenly stand out. In summer, that same animal can blend in so well that a whole summer passes without spotting a fox. In winter, seeing them becomes normal. The animals did not suddenly appear in winter. They were there all along. The difference was visibility.

That also tells me something about missed bears. Based on what has been seen and what others have pointed out, along with my fox evidence, a rough estimate is that, of the bears close enough to be seen, I still miss about half.

The number is not scientific. It is a field estimate built from my real misses, later confirmed by someone else.

A simple way to think about it is this:

* When hiking alone, only the bears that I notice get counted.

* When hiking with someone behind me, the bears that get pointed out become a glimpse into what would have been missed.

* Over time, those "friend-spotted" bears and my fox spotting evidence function like a sample, suggesting a larger number that never register at all.

Even if the estimate is wrong by a wide margin, the main truth remains: bears can be very close without being detected.

The stories that follow share one thing in common. These are all close bears I would have walked by and never known about without another set of eyes or looking back.

In all of these encounters, the bears did not respond as if a threat had arrived. They responded as if a quiet presence was passing through. I have come to believe that my own movement changes how I experience these moments.

Black Bear on Slough Creek

I was hiking up Slough Creek with my wife and a friend one morning in early June. We walked along, enjoying the Arrowleaf sunflowers growing thick everywhere. The people who hike with me know I tend to keep the hike quiet. Occasional quiet whispering is fine.

We passed a few small ponds full of water with ducks and other birds in and around them. Bison were scattered nearby, as they usually are, and some were close to the trail. My attention stayed on the trail ahead, and now and then, on the ponds. I was not watching the small rise right beside the trail on my left.

Suddenly I heard a voice from behind me, not loud, but louder than what is acceptable for me while hiking. I thought I heard, "Bear." I turned around and saw my wife pointing to a spot beside me that I had walked past. Sitting there in the green grass and sunflowers, no more than ten yards away, was a large black bear. It sat as if it were simply amused by the quiet line of people walking by.

I brought my camera up and started recording. In that moment, I do not recall any of us moving for bear spray. It was amazing how the bear sat there watching us while we watched it. After thirty seconds, it stood and began walking casually, first parallel to us, then angling away. During that slow walk, it looked back once, as if checking whether we were still there, and then disappeared over the small rise.

It was a bear which showed no aggression. It felt like the bear simply tolerated being noticed, sitting there still. Its behavior was like an animal waking from a deep sleep, needing a moment to gather itself before calmly moving off. It seemed at ease with our presence, and after that brief pause, it left.

What this showed me: A bear can sit ten yards away and remain unseen. In that moment, nothing escalated, and the quiet felt like part of the reason.

A Mother with a Cub

Mount Everts is the highest peak above the cliffs east of Mammoth. I have never seen another person hiking in the area. It is a beautiful place, and the amount of wildlife always leaves an impression on me. Elk, bison, bighorn sheep, wolves, coyotes, and bears are almost always part of the day. This is a place I hike once a year, usually in June.

There are no designated Yellowstone trails in this area, which is one reason it stays so empty of people. I was walking through scattered trees with snow patches and stretches of dry ground. It was not thick timber, and the visibility was good for watching wildlife.

I was moving along a slope beside those scattered trees and apparently walked right by a mother black bear with her cub. One habit I have is to turn and look behind me for this very reason. Many times, bears are spotted behind rather than ahead.

This time, when I turned around, the mother and cub were about thirty yards back. For a moment, I just stood there, amazed that I hadn't seen them. They had to have been right there beside the path I had taken, sitting still and unseen as I passed. The thought of it was almost hard to accept, not because it felt dangerous, but because it showed how easily bears can be present without being detected.

When I first noticed her, the mother was completely unalarmed by my presence. The two of them were out in the open, moving with the calm of animals that belonged there. The mother's attention stayed on the ground and on her cub, as if I did not exist. Now and then, she would lift her head and look around, not in panic, but in the steady way a mother checks her surroundings.

The cub didn't always stay close. It would spend time doing its own thing, then run to the mother before going off on its own again. It was being watched now and then by the mother.

For several minutes, they stayed within thirty to fifty yards, and the longer I watched them, the more it felt like I was being allowed to witness something private. The mother would nose through the grass for something to eat, and the cub would mimic her and then walk away.

After a few minutes I moved to at least 100 yards away, to what felt like a safer distance to observe them. Even then, the mother stayed at ease, focused on feeding, while the cub was off doing something else.

In the end, I was the one who moved off and continued my hike. By moving in a way that peacefully coexists with wildlife in their home can make my experience feel so amazing.

What this showed me: Even with good visibility, a bear and cub can be close and still go unnoticed. In this moment, the mother did not get upset, and I did not take that for granted.

The Grizzly that Walked Out Behind Me

I was walking early one morning. The sun was low in the east, and a dense line of timber ran close along my right side. Most of my attention stayed to the left, toward the open ground, watching for wildlife where the light was good. I gave little thought to the thick, dark timber.

It was hard to see any distance into the timber. Most of the time, nothing showed itself there. I kept moving, quiet and slow, observing the morning.

When I looked back, a grizzly bear came out of the trees behind me, about thirty yards away. It had waited for me to pass before moving out into the open. It appeared completely at ease, even that close. I had seen bears do this before, staying in cover until people passed, then stepping out and going on with their day.

The bear was not upset or agitated. It let me pass, then walked out behind me in plain sight and eased into the sagebrush. It started digging and grazing.

What this showed me: A bear may hold still in timber, let a person pass, then step out calmly. In this moment, the bear did not treat my presence as an immediate threat.

Two Grizzlies in the Dark

One early morning, before first light, I was hiking up a trail with a friend behind me. Because of the darkness, most of my attention stayed on the trail itself, watching where my boots landed so I did not step into a hole or catch a toe on a rock and stumble.

On mornings like this, I often hear movement near the trail. The sound might be a deer slipping through brush or something heavier shifting off the path in the dark. More than once, I have heard footsteps that seemed to angle away from the trail, keeping pace with me for a moment before fading out. On longer hikes in complete darkness, I have sometimes carried a thermal scope. I did not have it with me this morning.

We kept climbing at our normal pace, quiet and slow. Then I heard a few odd sounds behind me. They were not loud, but different from normal hiking noises. I turned and saw my friend standing and pointing to a place I had just passed.

Right there, about fifteen yards away, a grizzly was standing in the dark. It was close enough that the shape of its shoulders and head was clear, even without much light. By the time I turned, it had already begun to walk away. It did not rush. It simply eased away, steady and calm. If my friend had not seen it, I would have walked past and never have known it was there.

A few minutes later, as the bear kept moving away from us, we spotted another grizzly farther out in the open. The second bear was easier to see, even in the dim light, and it made the first encounter seem even more surprising. Two bears, both close, and one of them was almost missed at fifteen yards.

Neither bear ran. The first grizzly continued walking away in a calm, steady walk. The second bear kept moving and grazing farther out, unhurried. Both bears looked calm and kept their distance. Our pace stayed slow and quiet, and nothing about the moment seemed to push them. For the next fifteen or twenty minutes, we watched them at a distance as we continued along the trail.

Moments like that answer a question without needing much thought. Bears can be near the trail and never be seen. In partial darkness, even a large animal can stand close and blend in, especially when attention is on the ground and the next step. I have seen the same thing happen more than once, hiking with someone else, in daylight and in the dark. Without another set of eyes, the backcountry can seem empty when it is not.

What this showed me: Darkness increases how much gets missed, even at fifteen yards. And on a calm trail, calm often meets calm.

Max Follows a Bear

One morning, I was hiking with my little dog Max, a schnauzer. The trail ran with thick brush tight along one side and open ground on the other. That layout shows up again and again in the backcountry. One side can hide a lot, and the other can make a person relax without meaning to.

Max and I were enjoying the walk, and nothing felt near. Max would stop now and then to smell something while I kept moving. Then he would hurry and catch up, trotting along as if the whole place belonged to him.

At one point I turned around to check on him, and what I saw was surprising. Max was behind me on the trail, and right beside him was a black bear. They were walking in the opposite direction, only about fifteen yards back.

The bear was moving at an easy pace, not fast and not tense. Max was right on its tail, following along like it was the most normal thing to do. The bear did not look upset, and it simply kept walking, steady and calm, with Max tagging along behind.

I called Max back. He turned and came to me, and the bear never ran. It just continued down the trail at the same pace, never looking back, as calm as it had been from the first moment I saw it.

In moments like that, it is obvious that the bear had been close before I ever knew it. The brush along the trail can hide a large animal. A bear can stay hidden until after a person has passed, and then appear behind.

Max has been on plenty of hikes in grizzly country outside the park, and fortunately there have never been issues with bears. Once, while camping with Max asleep in the tent, I woke the next morning and found a bunch of things missing from camp. Some of it was scattered in an open area up to fifty yards away. I found black bear tracks about ten yards away on the trail, but I could not find any tracks inside the camp itself. Whatever hauled those things away did not bother Max. He never woke up, and I never heard a sound.

What this shows me: Calm movement helps keep everything calm for me. Again and again, bears seem to behave as if they are reading intent, often deciding there is nothing to fear, even before I know they are there.

A lot of what I grew up hearing about wilderness and wildlife trained my mind to brace for the worst. After years of walking alone in grizzly country, I still respect what these places can do, but my mind does not run on fear. I move through wild places with knowledge and experience, staying alert and calm. Freedom, for me, begins when fear is replaced by steady awareness.

Appendix:

Preparation Before Hike

People often ask how I prepare for a long hike, especially when I am hiking alone and traveling through grizzly country. What I do is not complicated, but it is deliberate. It starts the night before.

The Night Before

The night before a hike, I make sure everything is ready so that the morning is simple and unhurried.

I start with my electronics. I charge all batteries for both of my cameras, a GoPro and a Canon SX70. I also make sure my inReach satellite communicator is fully charged and ready. Before each hike, I check that it has the latest software loaded and is functioning properly. This is not something I rush or skip.

I mount my camera to the tripod so it is ready to use. I check my pack and make sure I have the amount of water I will need. There are items that always stay in my pack and do not require checking each time, such as a water filter, first aid kit, and a fire starter. I make sure to add snacks or small treats that I want to take with me, sometimes Oreo cookies or candy bars.

I lay out my clothing, boots, and gaiters so everything is in one place. I also keep an auxiliary bag that is always packed and ready. That bag includes a change of clothes, extra socks, extra coats, hand warmers, microspikes for icy trails, extra rain gear, and a towel. When the time comes, all I have to do is grab it.

I make sure the car is refueled and ready to go. Then I go to bed at least 8 hours before the time I need to get up. Sleep matters.

The Morning of the Hike

The morning routine depends on how far I need to drive. My drives range from 1.5 to 3 hours, one way. I get up at least 50 minutes before I need to leave. That gives me enough time to eat breakfast and load the car without rushing.

My wife also gets up with me. She makes me breakfast, usually eggs and toast, and prepares a lunch and hot chocolate for my pack. She also makes sure there is food and a drink waiting for me when I return to the car. That support matters more than most people realize.

As soon as I get in the car, I test my inReach to make sure it is working and communicating properly.

I always want to arrive at the trailhead at least 30 minutes before first light. For example, at the end of June, that means being at the trailhead between 4:00 and 4:15 A.M. If the drive is 3 hours, that means leaving home by 1:00 A.M., which in turn means getting up a little after midnight.

Why I Start So Early

There are several reasons I start hiking so early.

The main reason is wildlife. The best wildlife viewing and the richest sounds of the backcountry happen at first light and sunrise. That is when the country feels most alive. I like to be about a mile down the trail just as the sky is starting to brighten.

Another reason is travel. At that hour, there is usually zero traffic on the roads, making for a smooth drive. Road construction can still be an issue, but otherwise the roads are quiet.

I also start early because I do not want anyone hiking ahead of me. Even though most people do not hike as far as I do, I prefer not to have another group in front of me filling the trail with noise. Only once did someone start out ahead of me. A man wearing a bright headlamp began hiking about a minute before I did. I still went ahead with my hike, but I immediately moved off trail. That day I saw two grizzly bears and a very close black bear. Other than that one exception, I have never had anyone hiking ahead of me in the morning.

Starting early gives me quiet and space to move through the landscape without distraction, and the best chance to see wildlife. That matters to me, and it is why I begin every hike before first light.

Gear List

Day Hike Gear List - Pack Wt. 14 lbs.

Camera	Monocular
inReach communication	First Aid Kit
Water and Filter	Food
Phone	Money/Visa
Park Pass/Driver's License	Bear Spray
Neck Gaiter	Coats and Gloves
Microspikes for icy trail	Sunglasses
Flashlight	Mosquito Spray and Net
Leg Gaiters	Knife
Hand/Toe Warmers	Garbage Bag
Poncho & Rain Pants	Mirror
Spoon	Fire Starter

Backpacking List - includes day hike gear list, 23 lbs. total

Cooking Pans	Food Hanging Rope
Camp Stove	Gas
Socks	Sleeping Bag

Tent

Flying Insect Spray

FLIR Thermal Scope

Toothpaste and Brush

Map

Sleeping Pad

Batteries

Foldable Bucket

Pillow

Acknowledgement

I thank my sister-in-law, Mary Ellen Fitzgerald, whose lifelong love of language and history shaped many thoughtful conversations during the writing of this book. While the words are mine, her encouragement and perspective were invaluable.

Correspondence

Correspondence from readers is welcome at:

StanMillsWildlifeArt@gmail.com

www.ingramcontent.com/pod-product-compliance
Lightning Source LLC
Chambersburg PA
CBHW052217270326
41931CB00011B/2390